BENEATH THE SIEGE:

ECHOES OF WAR

AND

WHISPERS OF LOVE

Elizabeta Usto-Dacic

The Struggle for Existence and the Road to Freedom

Memoir

ISBN: 979-8-218-38114-1

Table of Contents

Elizabeta Usto-Dacic

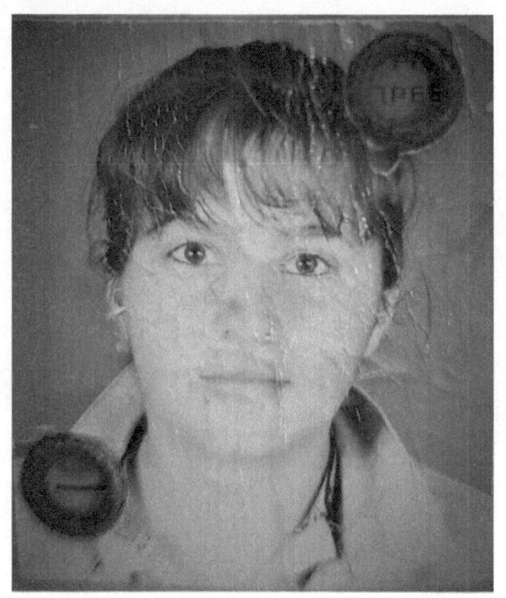

17-year-old Elizabeta.

Photo taken in Foca, Bosnia, few months before the war in 1992.

Dedication

This memoir serves as an honor to those who impacted my life and helped me become the person I am today. It is written with love, and remembrance of my two brothers, Ferid and Nedzad. Their absence is an empty space that time will never fill. These pages will forever witness their humor, bravery, honor, and love.

To my brave mother, Semsa

who sacrificed not one, but two sons for the country she loved.

THE BEGINNING:
APRIL 7TH, 1992, FOCA.

Today is the 3rd day of Eid. My neighborhood was filled with beautiful smells of homemade sweets, traditional Bosnian cuisine, and music. Out of nowhere, an eerie stillness had settled over my neighborhood. The atmosphere became tense, something I could sense in my body and bones. This quietness differs strikingly from the usual sounds of children's laughter, shouts, and playful commotion that filled our days. On this day, the sky was "heavy" and gray, mirroring the worrying mood surrounding us. Today should be a day for celebrations and visiting family, neighbors, and friends, but instead, parents were calling their children to rush inside.

I had just returned from a trip to the store, where I had gone to buy a new pair of shoes. Walking home, I couldn't help but notice the empty streets. These are the same streets that were usually bustling with the joyful chaos of kids playing. The unusual quietness was unsettling, filling me with a growing fear. I found myself anxiously wondering, "What's happening? Where is everyone?" The absence of familiar and lively sounds in the neighborhood concerned me, leaving me with more questions than answers. The urge to get home was overwhelming, and when I arrived, I immediately sensed the worry that seemed to engulf our home. I could see the concern on my mother's face. Her worries filled the room. The comfort of being home contrasted starkly against this uneasy atmosphere, making me aware of the situation unfolding around us. When she saw me, she uttered, "We have to go. Now." She barely spoke those words when a series of loud explosions began to echo through the neighborhood. We didn't know where these terrifying sounds came from, adding to the chaos and fear.

In the middle of the sudden eruption of explosions, my mom's voice cut through the confusion, her tone full of urgency as she yelled, "Let's go!" Her command left no room for hesitation. At that moment, the reality of the situation became apparent. We were in the middle of something dangerous beyond our understanding. In a moment of youthful naivety and defiance, I called my two younger sisters, urging them to follow Mom. I was reluctant to leave because I couldn't fully understand what was happening. I thought I would be safe at home. Part of me wanted to retreat into everyday life's normalcy, shower, wash my long hair, and try on the new shoes I had just bought. At 17, the gravity of the situation hadn't fully registered with me. I didn't fully comprehend that the explosions echoing in our neighborhood were announcing the onset of a conflict, a war that would stretch on for nearly four years. At that moment, caught between the innocence of youth and the brink of a crisis that would change my life, I struggled to reconcile my desire for simple comforts with the intensifying reality outside.

As the evening crept in, the sounds of gunfire and explosions grew more intense, shattering the remaining facade of normalcy. With each passing moment, my worry escalated into fear. Alone at home, with no clear destination or plan, I was engulfed by a sense of vulnerability. I decided to seek refuge in the basement attached to our house. It wasn't just an aimless choice; the cellar seemed the safest place in that chaos. When I got there, I realized I wasn't alone. Some of my neighbors had gathered there, seeking shelter from the unimaginable confusion. Among them were two seven-day-old babies, an a two-year-old boy. The boy was my brother's son. The sight of these innocent faces of the children starkly contrasted with the harrowing reality we were all pushed into. Their presence brought a new level of seriousness to the situation. It wasn't just about my safety anymore; it was about these vulnerable lives, which had barely begun and were now caught in a conflict they could not understand. The cramped and dimly lit basement suddenly transformed into a shelter, a cramped ark braving the storm of war that raged outside.

A loud explosion suddenly rocked the house, causing it to tremble as if caught in an earthquake's grip. The immediate aftermath was a loud sound of terror. The screams that followed were even more frightening than the shuddering of the walls around us. In that chaos, the cries of the babies pierced the air, mingling with the distressed sobs of their mothers.

In this confusion, my fears took a different shape. My thoughts raced to my mom and my sisters, who had left earlier to escape the escalating violence. Worry for their safety engulfed me, overshadowing my sense of danger. Were they safe? Had they found shelter? The uncertainty was unbearable. In that basement, surrounded by fear and distress, I felt a profound sense of helplessness. I wanted to comfort those around me, to reassure them, but the words felt empty against the backdrop of the war unfolding outside. All I could do was wait, hope, and worry as we huddled together, united by a shared vulnerability in the face of a conflict that had suddenly changed our lives.

The basement door suddenly opened, and a familiar voice pierced the tense air. It was one of my brothers. "Get out!" he yelled. He quickly explained that a projectile had hit our house, making it clear that the basement was no longer safe. As he continued to urge us to run, his voice grew more insistent, pushing everyone into action. "Fast and as far as possible," he instructed. The sound of gunfire seemed to intensify, creating a terrifying symphony that underscored his words, "They are getting closer." At that moment, there was no time for contemplation or hesitation. I sprang into action, following my brother's lead. I emerged from the basement into a world that seemed to have descended into chaos. The once-familiar streets were now corridors of the unknown and the danger. As I ran from the house, my mind was a whirlwind of fear and adrenaline. Each step was driven by a primal instinct to survive, to find safety in the storm of violence that had engulfed my neighborhood and my home.

The sounds of gunfire and warfare echoed around me, a reminder that every moment spent in indecision could be deadly. I ran as fast as I could, propelled by the urgency to escape, leaving behind the remnants of a life that had been shattered that day in the wake of a war that had come too close to home.

Tears streamed down my face as I ran, a mix of fear, desperation, and a profound sense of loss. The sound of bullets striking the ground was terrifyingly close, a relentless reminder of the danger I was in. In my panic, I called out for my mom, sisters, and brothers, clinging to the hope that they were nearby. I knew my mom wouldn't go far away from our home; why would she? That house was more than just walls and a roof. It was our labor of love, a witness to years of hard work and dreams. Now, in a twist of fate, we were being forced to abandon it, to flee from the place we had poured our hearts into. The thought of someone coming to burn our home was almost too much to bear. It was not just a physical structure under threat but a storage of our memories, joys, and struggles.

With every step I took away from it, I felt a piece of my history and identity stripped away. The reality of the situation was stark and brutal. Survival was now our only goal, and everything else, no matter how cherished, had to be left behind. In that frantic run, my mind raced with worry: where were my mother and sisters? Where are my brothers? Are they safe? The ambivalence was unbearable. The sounds of the war raged a grim backdrop to the personal turmoil I was experiencing. In those moments, the world seemed to have narrowed down to the basic survival instinct, and each step became a bid to escape the chaos that had erupted around us.

And just like that, without any warnings or preparation, my life took a turn I could never have imagined. In the blink of an eye, I transformed from a teenager with everyday concerns and joys to a refugee, uprooted and pushed into a dangerous journey. At 17, when my biggest worries should have been about love, school, and friends, I grappled with a harsh new reality and the question of "how to survive a war?"

******

April 7th, 1992 marked the beginning of a struggle for survival, a date etched into my memory as the day everything changed. The familiar rhythms of my life were shattered, replaced by an urgent need to navigate a world turned upside down by conflict. This was the beginning of a displacement and a profound alteration of my identity and future.

As I ran from the only home I had ever known, with the sounds of war echoing behind me, I stepped into the unknown. The road ahead was fraught with challenges and dangers but also a path of resilience and strength. It was the start of a journey that would test and shape me in ways I could never have anticipated. My story as a refugee, a 17-year-old girl forced to confront the realities of war, was beginning.

Through the tears that blurred my vision, the glimmer of house lights began to emerge in the distance. A beacon of hope, they seemed to promise safety and a reprieve from the chaos. My thoughts were singular: run and keep running. Every fiber of my being was focused on reaching those houses, even as I continued to call out desperately for my mom and siblings.

Then, suddenly, a familiar voice cut through the night, "We are here. Stop yelling!" My younger brother's voice was a balm to my frayed nerves. There, in the dim light, were my mom and sisters. Overwhelmed with relief, I sprinted towards them as my heart pounded with fear and gratitude.

As we huddled together, I couldn't help but ask, "Where are the others?" My thoughts immediately turned to my two other brothers, especially the eldest. The confusion regarding his whereabouts sent me a wave of worry. During our reunion, his absence was a reminder of the fragility of our situation. Each of us was grappling with our fears and anxieties, yet united in the hope that somehow, in all this craziness, we would find safety together. At that moment, the reality of our circumstances was inescapable. We were a family fragmented by war, each carrying the burden of concern for the others. As the night pressed on, the question of my oldest brother's safety hung heavy, symbolizing the troubles ahead.

We reached the village. The scene that unfolded before us was one of stark, raw humanity in the face of crisis. People were everywhere, their faces etched with fear, confusion, and exhaustion. Most were empty-handed, having fled with nothing but the clothes on their backs. Mothers clutched their babies tightly. Among the crowd, I noticed a few men armed with guns. Recognizing them brought a sense of familiarity and slightly easing my fear. They weren't strangers. They were faces I knew, part of the community, and they were here to protect us. This image offered a small comfort in this chaos.

As I looked around, the moonlight cast a bright, surreal glow over the scene, illuminating the faces of those I recognized. Some were neighbors, other acquaintances from the village. Their expressions spoke volumes. Fear had taken hold, and the anxiety about the future was palpable. Children's cries pierced the night, adding to the somber atmosphere. People sat on the ground, perhaps too weary of standing or simply in shock from the rapid unraveling of their lives. In this village, under the moon's watchful eye, we had become a collective of displaced souls, each person grappling with the sudden upending of their world. We were all refugees now, bound together by the shared experience of having our lives turned upside down in the blink of an eye.

A peaceful calm settled over the village as the hours slowly ticked by. The earlier panic and chaos gave way to a heavy stillness, punctuated only by the occasional distant sound. Exhaustion took its toll, and one by one, the children succumbed to sleep, their cries fading into silent, fitful slumbers. My sisters had found their way to sleep, nestled somewhere safe under our mother's watchful eye. She had taken them under her care, ensuring they were as comfortable as possible, given the circumstances. Their absence left me in a solitary vigil, sitting outside, exposed to the cool night air. Under the dim light of the stars, I waited for my oldest brother. His whereabouts were still unknown, and that weighed heavily on my heart. The quiet of the night seemed to amplify my worries, each passing moment stretching into an eternity of concern and hope.

That night, the simple act of waiting became a test of patience and resilience. It was a solitary experience despite being surrounded by others. In our way, we grappled with personal fears and anxieties, even as we shared the bond of displacement and worry. My gaze often drifted to the paths leading into the village as I sat there with a silent plea for his safe return and hope that our family would reunite.

Sleep avoided me entirely that night. I found myself rooted in the dirt road, my eyes fixated on the hiking paths leading into the village, holding onto the hope of seeing my brother. The world around me was shrouded in the quiet darkness of the night.

As the first light of dawn began to creep over the horizon, a gentle fog rose, blanketing the surroundings in a surreal haze. In this ethereal morning light, I saw them – two feet, approaching slowly through the mist. There was something unmistakably familiar about the way they moved. A surge of recognition coursed through me; it was my brother's walk. Overcome with relief, joy, and lingering frustration, I jumped and ran towards him. My voice, laden with a night's worth of worry, echoed through the quiet morning air as I yelled, "Where were you all night?"

Seeing him, a reassuring presence amid the chaos, brought many emotions. The fear of the unknown that had gripped me all night began to disappear, replaced by the overwhelming relief of reunion. In that moment, the significance of family, the bond that had held firm even through the distress of war, was more evident than ever. With my brother's return, our small family was together again, bringing an indescribable sense of comfort in the chaos.

As the village slowly stirred to life in those early hours, there was a shift in the atmosphere. People began emerging from their temporary shelters, with a sense of urgency evident in their movements. The community was awakening to a new day and the harsh reality that we could no longer stay here. Whispers and hurried conversations filled the air as everyone prepared to leave. The news that the Serbian army forces had taken over our city and were advancing towards this village spread rapidly, fueling a sense of imminent danger. This small village was no longer a place of refuge; it had become another point in the path of the encroaching conflict.

In the face of this escalating danger, I returned to my house one last time. Despite the risks, the need to retrieve some personal belongings, my purse, hairbrush, and perhaps some clothes, felt crucial, a small way to hold onto a fragment of my former life. I left for my house without informing anyone, driven by determination and fear. The village, now a hive of hurried departures, remained oblivious to my detour. Once inside my house, a place that embodied safety and familiarity, I was overwhelmed by a sense of urgency. The reality of the situation was all too apparent. I quickly grabbed my purse, not bothering to check what was inside, and my hairbrush. I thought of gathering clothes, but fear overpowered me; lingering in the house felt increasingly dangerous. With a heart pounding as a ticking clock, in danger, I escaped through the bathroom window and ran the same route I had taken the night before.

As I returned to the village, the realization dawned on me with heartbreaking clarity: this was a final farewell to my home. The place that nurtured me in the last ten years and witnessed our joys and sorrows was now part of a past that I must leave behind. At that moment, I understood that there was no going back. The path ahead was full of doubt, a journey away from the remnants of a life that could no longer be. The final glimpse of my home, receding in the distance, symbolized the loss and change that had become the new constants in my life.

The decision to evacuate was not just a strategic move for safety; it was a painful acknowledgment of our vulnerability in this escalating war. Families, friends, and neighbors are now united. There is only one goal: survival. The idea of an everyday life had vanished, replaced by the necessity to keep moving and stay one step ahead of the conflict consuming our homeland. As we gathered a few of our belongings, the reality of our situation was apparent. We were not just leaving a village. We were leaving behind a part of ourselves, our history, and our connection to a place we once called home. The question of where we were going was not important anymore because of the immediate need to escape the danger that was drawing closer. In those moments, as we joined the stream of people setting out on a questionable journey, there was a silent, collective resolve. We were more than just displaced individuals; we were a community bound by a shared ordeal.

As we embarked on foot, leaving the village behind in the cold light of dawn, the distant sound of gunfire grew closer. The air, chilling with each passing moment, soon carried the soft flutter of snowflakes, adding a surreal quality to our grim exodus. Packed with people who were fortunate enough to have them, cars sped past us, engines a muffled roar against the crunch of snow underfoot. We had no choice but to keep walking. The limited resources and the suddenness of our departure meant that many of us were left to rely on our strength and resilience. The snow, gently falling, seemed inconsistent with the sense of danger rapidly closing in.

Several villagers had decided to stay behind, trusting in the hope that they would be safe. It was a hope that we later learned was tragically misplaced. The Yugoslavian army, which was supposed to be a source of protection, turned against them. The news of their deaths reached us like a cold wind, cutting through the already bleak reality we faced. This revelation casts a dark shadow over our journey as it reminded us of the brutality of war and the fragility of life within it. The feeling of helplessness was overwhelming, knowing that those we had left behind had met such a cruel fate.

As we trudged through the snow, each step was heavy, with physical exhaustion, the weight of loss, and the fear of what lay ahead. Our path was unsure, our future unclear, but we were driven by the need to survive, to find safety in a world where the familiar had been replaced by the unpredictable and dangerous.

Our journey took on a new focus: reaching Sarajevo, the capital of Bosnia, by any means necessary, even if it meant traversing the distance on foot. The city held more than just the promise of refuge; it was where some of my mother's family lived, offering a glimmer of hope in reuniting with loved ones and finding some semblance of safety. The direct road distance to Sarajevo was about 72 kilometers, but our path was far longer and harder. We had to navigate through rugged terrain, following hiking trails that meandered over mountains, a route significantly more prolonged and challenging than any paved road. The journey, we knew, would span several days, a test of endurance and resolve. Undeterred, we set out, moving from one village to the next. Each day brought challenges and small victories as we slowly but steadily progressed. The route was physically and emotionally exhausting, but our determination did not waver. The landscape around us was a mix of familiar and unfamiliar scenes that reminded us of the life we once knew.

Eventually, our journey brought us to Gorazde, a city we had visited many times. The town, with the river Drina cutting gracefully through it, was beautiful. Seeing Gorazde under these circumstances was a surreal experience. The city, once a destination for joyful visits, is now a milestone in our arduous journey. Standing on the outskirts of Gorazde, memories of our previous visits flooded back. The city, with its familiar landscapes and the gentle flow of the Drina, offered a brief respite for our weary spirits. Yet, even in this moment of relative calm, our goal remained clear: to reach Sarajevo and hopefully find a safe place in a world turned upside down. Gorazde stood as a beacon of fragile liberty in all the turmoil. Although it was a "free" city, not yet occupied by Serbian forces, the reality of its situation was evident. The town was effectively besieged and encircled by hostile forces. The daily sound of gunfire served as a reminder that freedom was hanging by a thread. We couldn't stay there for long and had to keep going. The decision to leave Gorazde was as inevitable as it was heart-wrenching.

The city, aware of the looming threat, had organized a convoy to help refugees escape to Sarajevo. However, the conditions of this evacuation were stark: only women, children, and older people were allowed on the buses. This meant that my brothers would have to stay behind. The thought of leaving them was unbearable. I wanted to stay, to face whatever came our way together as a family, but my mother was adamant. She insisted that my sisters and I take this chance to reach Sarajevo, where our uncle awaits us. My brother's promise that they would follow as soon as possible did little to ease the ache in my heart.

Boarding the bus, I was overwhelmed with emotions. Tears streamed down my face as the reality of the situation sank in. I was leaving part of my family behind in a city ringed with danger, stepping into the unknown. The separation was painful and mixed with a haunting suspicion, an unspoken fear that this might be the last time I would see my brothers.

As the bus pulled away, carrying me and so many others towards an uncertain road ahead, I gazed out of the window, the image of my brothers standing in the crowd etched into my memory, forever.

THE THEFT OF HOPE

The bus journey to Sarajevo was a long, sad procession through a landscape scarred by war. The roads, once familiar, now carried a sense of foreboding, each mile taking us further from what had been our life. Around me, the bus filled with faces marked by the same mix of fear, anxiety, and a faint glimmer of hope. Mothers tried to soothe their children, some too young to understand the danger we got caught in. Older people sat in stoic silence, their eyes reflecting the sorrow of leaving their homes and families, perhaps for the last time.

As we traveled, the conversation among the passengers was sparse, often calm, as if speaking too loudly might disturb the fragile veil of calm. Every so often, the bus would lurch to a stop, the sound of distant shelling a grim reminder of the war raging around us. We would hold our breath, praying to remain unnoticed by the conflict's ever-reaching arms.

As our convoy of five buses full of refugees wound its way across the plateau of Romanija, drawing closer to Sarajevo, a heavy sense of anticipation filled the air. Our journey, fraught with uncertainty and the shadows of war, had been extended. But just when we thought we were nearing our destination, the buses began to slow, eventually grinding to a halt. The abrupt stop sent a ripple of unease through us all.

The doors of the bus swung open, breaking the tense silence. Armed men, their faces stern and unyielding, stormed in. Their shouts pierced the air, "Leave everything and get out!" The command was stark, brooking no argument. We complied, one by one, stepping out into the unknown, our hearts pounding with fear and resentment. Lined up next to the buses, an eerie sense of vulnerability engulfed us. We watched helplessly as these armed intruders plundered our last possessions. They ransacked the buses with ruthless efficiency, seizing food, clothing, and even the precious milk meant for the babies and children. They took every item that represented a sliver of comfort or survival. The sight of them carrying away these essentials, things that meant the difference between sustenance and hunger, was a harsh blow.

After they stripped the buses of everything valuable, they ordered us to return inside. Re-entering the bus, the cold barrels of their guns felt like silent, menacing spectators, reminding us of our vulnerability and their power. The theft of our belongings was not just a loss of physical items; it was a theft of dignity, a stark reminder of the cruelty and heartlessness that war breeds.

As the buses started moving again, a heavy silence settled among us. The loss we had just experienced was more than the sum of the items taken; it was a profound reminder of the fragility of our situation. Yet, amidst this safety and security violation, a quiet determination kindled within us. We were more than the sum of our possessions, more than the victims of this war. Even though they had taken much, they could not take away our unyielding spirit to persevere.

The buses continued steadily ahead, away from the roadblock and armed men. The landscape outside shifted gradually, from rural countryside to the more rugged terrain that signaled our approach to Sarajevo. The city, once a vibrant metropolis known for its cultural diversity and historical significance, was now the epicenter of the conflict. As we neared, the signs of war became increasingly evident: buildings and houses marked with bullet holes, the remnants of shelled structures, and the occasional sight of military vehicles or armed personnel. Still on the bus, clutching my sisters' hands tightly, I scanned the crowd for our uncle, but he was not in the waiting for us. In all those faces, I searched for a familiar connection to our family and life, the life we had to leave behind.

In those first moments in Sarajevo, our reality was overwhelming. We were refugees in our own country, reliant on the kindness of relatives and the scarce resources in the city under siege. The journey ahead was unclear, but the resilience that had carried us this far remained unbroken. Sarajevo, a town bearing the scars of war, was now our refuge, a place to rebuild and hold onto hope in a nation torn apart.

THE ENEMY BOMBARDS SARAJEVO

May 2nd, 1992 marked a day I would never forget. Sarajevo, the city already steeped in the shadow of war, greeted us with a jarring welcome. As our bus slowly made its way through the streets, a sudden roar filled the air. The noise increased, a sound of terror that sent a wave of panic through everyone on board. Frantic voices rose in a chorus of fear as we all strained to identify the source of the ominous sound. In a split second, the bus driver slammed the brakes so violently that many of us got thrown from our seats. Outside, the horrifying reality became clear: an enemy airplane was swooping over the city, its bombs raining down with deadly intent. Air filled with explosions, chaos, and the terrifying sounds of destruction. Immediately, he orders everyone to evacuate the bus and seek shelter. There was no time for hesitation; survival was the only thing that mattered. As we disembarked, the streets were already teeming with people, a mix of residents and fellow refugees. We were united in a desperate scramble for safety.

My sisters, with their faces etched with fear, clung to me tightly. At 15 and 12, they were too young to fully understand the gravity of our situation, yet old enough to feel the terror buzzing in the air. We had nothing with us, no belongings to weigh us down, only each other. In all this chaos, a stranger's gesture became our lifeline. He waved at us frantically, urging us to run towards him. With no time to think, we followed his lead. He quickly ushered us into his house. Inside, the stranger's home became a temporary haven. The walls muffled the sounds of the war outside, providing shelter from the immediate danger. In those moments, the kindness of this stranger was a sharp contrast to the violence and hatred that is destroying our country. His swift action to shelter us, three frightened girls he had never met before, was proof of the enduring spirit of humanity, even in the darkest of times.

Surviving that day in Sarajevo felt like a miracle. Hiding in the basement of a stranger's house, we found ourselves in a surreal world far away from the life we once knew. The lack of electricity sunken us into darkness, and the absence of running water was a grim reminder of the city's under siege conditions. Yet, in that basement lit by a candle, there was a sense of solidarity among us, a shared determination to persevere. The homeowners, whose faces were wrapped with worry and fatigue I felt, generously shared their little food with us. It was the first meal we had eaten since leaving Gorazde, and though it was simple, it was a profound act of kindness in such dire times. Each bite was a reminder of the humanity that persisted even as the world outside crumbled under the weight of conflict. My thoughts wandered to my family, brothers, and mother as we ate: "Where are they? Are they safe?" The ambivalence was unbearable. I replayed our last moments together over and over in my mind, clinging to the hope that they had found some refuge from the violence. The not knowing was the most challenging part, each passing hour stretching into an eternity of worry.

In that basement, it seemed that the time stood still. We were a group of strangers brought together by circumstance, bound by the common goal of survival. The sounds of the war outside occasionally penetrated our temporary shelter, a reminder of the danger we are in. In those moments, the kindness of our hosts and the shared fears and hopes created a bond that transcended the horrors unfolding around us. As night fell, the basement's darkness was both a comfort and a challenge, cloaking us in safety and the unknown. My mind was restless, concerned about my family's well-being and our future. But amid all the fear and anxiety, there was a glimmer of something resilient and hopeful within me, a determination to survive, to reunite with my family, and to hold onto the belief that better days lay ahead.

Despite the overwhelming exhaustion that clung to every part of my being, sleep remained elusive that night. Each time I closed my eyes, the barrage of fears and 'what-ifs' marched relentlessly through my mind. The responsibility I felt for my sisters weighed heavily on me. I was their elder, their protector in this chaos, and I couldn't afford to show my fear. They looked to me for strength, and I was determined not to disappoint them.

The basement, our makeshift sanctuary, was constantly filled with the sounds of war. Explosions rumbled in the distance. A sinister lullaby that kept us awake. The gunfire, sometimes distant and sometimes frighteningly close, punctuated the night. We lay there, each lost in our thoughts, as these sounds of conflict became the soundtrack of our new reality. I constantly checked on my sisters, ensuring they were safe and comfortable. Their occasional whimpers in their sleep made my heart clench with pity and an intensified sense of protectiveness as time wrapped the basement in the darkness, stretching out endlessly. My thoughts often drifted to my brothers and my mother, their whereabouts a constant source of anxiety. I hoped that they were somewhere safe.

That night was a profound test of endurance. It wasn't just about surviving the physical threat of the war outside; it was also about battling the inner turmoil and the fear that threatened to overwhelm me. I had to stay strong, not just for my own sake, but for my sisters who depended on me. In the face of adversity, I discovered a resilience within myself I never knew I had. The night was long and fraught with danger, but we made it through.

Stepping out into Sarajevo's eerily quiet morning, I felt a deceptive calm. The relentless sound of gunfire had ceased, leaving an unsettling and hopeful silence. Was it temporary, or had something changed the course of the war? Questions swirled in my mind, each as confusing as the next.

Driven by a need to connect with my family, I set out to find a working phone. The necessity to inform my brother of our arrival in Sarajevo, to assure him of our safety, was pressing. After asking a few neighbors, I finally found an operational phone. My heart raced as I dialed the number, each ring amplifying my anxiety. When my brother answered, a wave of mixed emotions washed over me. I was relieved to hear his voice and confused by the mix of anger, anger at being sent away and being separated from my family in such a tumultuous time. His attempt at lightening the mood with a joke about visiting Sarajevo fell flat. I couldn't mask my anger, and my tone must have conveyed my feelings more than I realized. Sensing my distress, he quickly shifted to a more serious note, promising that they, he, my mom, and my younger brother, would make their way to Sarajevo on foot. It was a promise filled with hope yet tinged with the uncertainty of our situation.

Little did I know, as I clung to his words, that this conversation would be our last. His promise that day, a beacon of hope in our lives, would remain unfulfilled. Unbeknownst to me, this phone call would become a memory I would hold onto in the years to come, the final connection to a brother whose voice, laughter, and presence would soon become echoes of a past abruptly and tragically severed by the ravages of war.

At that moment, standing with the receiver in hand, I was unaware of the painful journey of loss that lay ahead. The promise of reunion, so earnestly made, would linger in my heart as a symbol of hope and love that persists even in the darkest times.

THE UNKNOWN

In the days that followed the conversation with my brother, unpredictability became our companion in Sarajevo. The city, once bustling with life, now echoed with the sounds of a siege, daily sounds of gunfire, the wail of sirens, and the warnings to remain indoors. The war had transformed our existence into a surreal landscape of fear and scarcity. The food we once took for granted became a luxury. Every morsel we found was a small victory against the hunger gnawed at us relentlessly. Amidst this and Sarajevo in fear, we would often reflect whether we would see the dawn of a new day.

In this chaos, I found myself in an unfamiliar role. With my mom and older brothers gone, I became the sole guardian of my two younger sisters. My youngest sister, merely 12 years old, clung to me constantly. In her eyes, I was her protector, her source of comfort and assurance in a world that had turned upside down. Her reliance on me was both a burden and a driving force, propelling me to find the strength I wasn't sure I had. A survival routine marked our days: scavenging for food, securing our shelter, and trying to maintain normalcy for my sisters' sake. We spent our nights huddled together, whispering stories of better times, hoping to drown out the sounds of war outside.

In those moments, I thought about my brothers and mother, and always wondering where they were and if they were safe. The lack of information and the inability to communicate added to the torment of our situation. Yet, in the face of all this, I had to remain strong, not just for my own sake but for my sisters, who looked up to me as their anchor in this storm. This period of our lives was a harsh lesson in the realities of war. It stripped away the innocence of my youth and forced me into a role I was unprepared for. But within this crucible of conflict, I discovered a resilience and a capacity for hope that I never knew I possessed. Like many in Sarajevo during those times, my story is one of endurance, of finding light in the darkest times, and of the powers of the human spirit.

As the months wore on, the absence of any news from my mom and brothers weighed heavily on my heart. Each day without a word from them has deepened the void of worry. However, we gradually learned to navigate the brutal realities of living in a war-torn city. Sarajevo, once vibrant, was now a landscape of survival, where the simplest tasks had become complex undertakings. The lack of electricity was one of the many challenges we faced, but the resilience of the human spirit shone through even in this darkness. Ingenious residents cobbled together makeshift generators, not for luxury but for a more crucial purpose – to power radios. These devices became our windows to the outside world, our only link to understanding the country's broader situation.

Radios crackled to life in dimly lit basements, where huddled groups clung to every word of the news broadcasts. Music, once a regular feature of radio channels, had given way to continuous updates and news. These broadcasts were our lifelines, offering snippets of information about other cities, like ours, under siege and surrounded by the enemy. But it was the end of these broadcasts that was the most heart-wrenching: the announcers would solemnly read the names of those killed in various parts of Bosnia, and in those moments, time seemed to stand still. People gathered around the radios, holding their breath, and prayed for their loved ones, hoping their names wouldn't be called. There was a collective relief when a familiar name wasn't mentioned, but the grief for those who weren't so fortunate was enormous.

For my sisters and me, these moments were a grim reminder of our situation. Each name read aloud represented a family irreversibly changed, much like ours. Our hearts ached not only for our family but for all those who had lost loved ones. This shared experience of loss and uncertainty created an unspoken bond among us all, a bond forged in the crucible of conflict.

Living through this time, my sisters and I clung to each other and the hope that our family would be reunited. This hope was a flickering flame that sustained us in the darkest hours. Our story, which echoed in the lives of countless others in Sarajevo, is a covenant to endurance, the strength of familial bonds, and the unyielding resilience of human spirit.

A FAREWELL

June 1992. A day that I had feared since the war began. Huddled around the radio in a dimly lit room, my sisters and I listened intently as the announcer started reading the names of those killed in Gorazde. This list bore the heaviest news imaginable. Amidst the names, one struck us like a lightning bolt, it was our brother's name. At that moment, time has stopped. My voice disappeared into a void of shock and disbelief. It was as if the air had been sucked out of the room, leaving us in a vacuum of despair. My sisters' faces mirrored my horror; their broad, tearful eyes looked to me for some semblance of hope or explanation. Our worst nightmare was unfolding right before us. In a desperate attempt to shield them from the crushing weight of this news, I found myself grasping at straws of hope. "It might be a mistake," I whispered in a voice barely audible, "Or perhaps someone else with the same name." I knew in my heart that such coincidences were rare, but I needed to offer some comfort, however small, to my sisters.

The possibility that our brother, our protector and guiding light, could be gone was too much to bear. The reality of war had always been brutal, but this was a personal tragedy that cut through the heart of our family. It was a loss that transcended the fear and anxiety we had been living with; it was a deep, personal wound to our very being.

As tears began to flow freely, I wrapped my arms around my sisters. We huddled together, each lost in a sea of grief and disbelief. In that darkened room, with only the static of the radio for company, we mourned not just our brother but the life we had known, a life now irretrievably altered by the cruelty of war.

In the days that followed, I struggled to maintain a façade of strength for my sisters, even as my own heart was shattered. Our brother's death was a stark reminder of the fragility of life during conflict, a reminder that the war was not just a series of events happening around us but a devastating force that had now torn our family apart. Our story, steeped in loss and resilience, became a testimonial of the enduring spirit of those who face the unthinkable yet find the strength to carry on.

The following day, propelled by desperation and faint hope, I went to the government officials to verify the devastating news. The journey felt surreal, each step heavy with dread and a sliver of hope that it was all a terrible mistake. But upon arriving and checking the list, it was confirmed: my brother's name was there. He was indeed gone. The reality of his death hit me with a force more significant than the initial shock of hearing his name on the radio. It was a confirmation I had dreaded, yet part of me had needed to see for myself to know for sure.

Walking back to the house where the kind stranger had taken us in, I was in a whirlwind of grief and confusion. The pain was a physical presence, a weight that seemed to grow with every step. "What do I do now? Where do we go from here? Is the rest of my family still alive?" These questions circled in my mind, each one echoing the profound uncertainty of our lives.

A deeper, more existential questioning surfaced in this turmoil: "Should I continue to live, and if so, for what?" The loss of my brother, the relentless war, the constant fear, it all seemed too much to bear. My role as the guardian of my sisters was the only thread holding me to life, but even this felt fragile in the face of such overwhelming sorrow. As I walked, the sounds of gunfire and chaos intensified, yet I felt invincible to the danger. The will to survive, once a powerful force, had dimmed in the shadow of my brother's death. I moved through the streets slowly, disconnected from the war-torn world around me, lost in a fog of grief.

Upon returning to the house, I was met with the worried faces of my sisters and our host. They were my remaining anchors to this world, the reasons I had to find a way to persevere despite the pain. In their eyes, I saw concern for me and a reflection of our shared loss and the collective need to find a way forward. In those moments and the days that followed, I grappled with the pain of loss and the necessity to keep going, not just for my sake but for my sisters, who depended on me. Our journey through the heart of darkness was far from over, but even in the depths of despair, the faintest glimmer of hope and the unbreakable bond of family guided us forward.

The Author is the owner of this photo.

My older brother Ferid.

IN THE SHADOW OF WAR

Death, once a distant concept, had become a daily occurrence in Sarajevo. It no longer carried the shock or the sting of the unexpected; it was our new, grim reality. The enemy, relentless in their cruelty, seemed determined to inflict as much harm as possible, aiming to break the spirit of every Bosnian. In this city under siege, every step outside our makeshift sanctuary was a gamble with fate. Once bustling with the energy of daily life, the streets had transformed into corridors of danger. The threat of a grenade or a projectile, or being shot from a sniper loomed constantly, making even the simplest tasks difficult and dangerous. We lived in a state of heightened alert, always anticipating the subsequent explosion, the next shattering of what little peace we could find.

The very concept of peace had become strange to us. It was a world that seemed to belong to another time, another life. The singular goal of survival consumed our days and nights. Each morning, we awoke not with thoughts of what the day might bring but with the question: "How can we stay alive today?"

In these dark times, our small home became a fortress of sorts. The stranger who had taken us in, whose name we learned was Amir, had become a guardian angel. His home was humble, yet it offered something invaluable: a refuge from the relentless bombardment and a sense of human connection amidst the dehumanizing brutality of war. Much like my lost brother, Amir had stepped into our protector role. He navigated the dangerous trips for food and essentials, always insisting on going alone to minimize our risk. His return each time was a small victory, a moment of relief and gratitude in our precarious existence.

The rhythm of the war dictated our daily routine. We learned to discern the sounds of different weapons to gauge the safety of venturing out based on the intensity of the fighting. We became experts in finding the safest corners of the house during gunfire, in making meals out of anything we could find, and in comforting each other during the endless nights filled with the sounds of gunfire and explosions.

As the weeks turned into months, I reflected on our serious situation. Here we were, three sisters, once concerned with love, school, friends, and the small joys of life, now living in a constant state of fear and survival. Our world had shrunk to an existence between the walls of a small house in a besieged city and our lives suspended in doubtfulness. Yet, even under these circumstances, there were moments of human connection, of shared resilience that gave us hope. The bond with Amir, the solidarity with other residents of Sarajevo, and the unspoken understanding between us all provided a sense of community. These connections were our lifeline, a reminder that even in the darkest times, the human spirit finds a way to seek light, hold on to hope, and fight for survival.

A BITTERSWEET REUNION

The refugee camp in Sarajevo had found its unlikely home in the college dorms, a place once bustling with the dreams and aspirations of domestic and international students. Now, these halls echoed with a different kind of story, one of displacement and survival. The students found themselves stranded in the dorms that had become a refuge for people fleeing from the neighboring towns, each carrying their tale of loss and resilience.

Frequent visits to the camp became a part of my routine. Those visits became ritual driven by the slim hope of finding my mother in the sea of people. Each trip was a mixture of hope and dread that ended in a quiet, sad walk back with a heart heavy from disappointment. But a figure caught my eye one day as I approached the entrance gate. Sitting alone and almost blending into the background, I spotted a familiar face. The feelings of disbelief and recognition washed over me. It was my middle brother. I yelled out his name with so much emotion that it filled the air and startled him. He looked at me, and the distance between us disappeared at that moment as he ran towards me. Our reunion was a tornado of tears, relief, and a thousand unspoken questions. This unexpected encounter felt like a ray of light in my life's darkness. My joy was short-lived, drowned by the sad news he brought. With a heavy heart, he told me that our younger brother has been killed, a loss that came barely two months after the death of our older brother. The news struck me with the force of a physical blow. I felt my legs give way beneath me as I crumpled to the ground. The weight of this latest tragedy was too much to bear. The loss of two brothers in such a short time was a harsh reality to comprehend. It felt as if our family, which was once full of life and love, was being dismantled by the merciless hands of war. As we stood there in the chaos of the refugee camp, our reunion took on a bittersweet tone.

While I was grateful that I had found my brother, the joy was tainted by the sorrow of our shared loss. We were two siblings united in grief, trying to make sense of a world that had gone crazy. At that moment, I realized that the war had changed our family forever. The innocence of our youth was gone, replaced by the harsh lessons of loss and survival. Yet, even in the depths of despair, our bond stood firm. This moment was a demonstration of our family's resilience, which will continue to be tested as we navigate the dangerous days ahead.

******

FRAGMENTS OF A FRACTURED FAMILY

The revelation that my brother had been in Sarajevo all this time, unaware of our presence, added another layer to our complex experiences during the war. His arrival was unexpected, a twist of fate in our fragmented family story. He had been hospitalized for months, recovering from injuries sustained in a harrowing escape attempt from Foca to Gorazde. The harshness of war was etched deeply into his being, visible in his physical appearance and the haunted look in his eyes. Leading him to the house where I had found shelter with my sisters, I braced myself for their reaction. The shock was evident as they struggled to recognize this drastically changed version of our brother. The brother they remembered was now hidden behind the facade of a man who had endured too much. His once robust frame was now gaunt, his clothes dirty and tattered, and his face marked by the rough growth of an unshaven beard.

As we sat together in the dim light of the room, a semblance of our old family unit, we began to exchange stories and information, pieces of our journeys during the war. It was a sad gathering, each tale punctuated by the heavy weight of loss and survival. My brother recounted his experience in the hospital, the pain, and the struggle to heal not just physically but emotionally. The most heart-wrenching part of his story was about our mother. She was still in Gorazde, trapped by the siege that had turned our hometown into a war zone. The knowledge that she was still out there, alone and in danger, was a hard pill to swallow. It reignited the helplessness and frustration that had become our constant companions.

Our conversation was an exchange of words and a shared grieving process. We mourned not only for our brothers who were no longer with us but for the life we had lost, the peace that seemed like a distant memory. Despite the reunion with my brother, the joy was incomplete, overshadowed by the absence of our mother and the worry surrounding her fate.

As we sat together that evening, there was a silent acknowledgment among us. We were survivors, each carrying our scars and stories, bound by blood and shared experiences. The road ahead was still unclear and fraught with challenges, but at that moment, having a part of my family by my side gave me a renewed strength to face whatever lay ahead. The war had taken much from us, but it had not succeeded in breaking our spirit.

ANOTHER FAREWELL

A year it had slipped by, marked by the relentless passage of war. Each day was a fight to survive, and a waiting game for any news of our mother. But silence was our only answer, a void filled with unspoken fears and fading hopes. The time has come to say goodbye to the house that had been our sanctuary for the past year. The family who had taken us in and shared their home and resources in these dire times had become more than just benefactors; they had become our extended family in a world where such bonds were often the difference between life and death.

The enemy's advance was inching closer to our part of town, a creeping shadow that forced everyone to abandon their homes. The sense of safety nurtured carefully in this house was uprooted, making us seek refuge elsewhere. Our destination was the makeshift refugee camp in the college dorms, which had become a collective shelter for many like us. We had little to take with us, just the clothes on our backs. The scarcity of necessities had been a constant, and the impending move reminded us of how little belongings we possessed.

On the day of our departure, emotions ran high. Leaving the house felt like leaving a part of ourselves behind, another fragment of stability lost to the chaos of war. The family we were leaving behind gathered to see us off, their faces etched with sadness and concern. In a gesture of kindness, they packed some food for us, mostly homemade bread, a simple and profound gift that would sustain us in more ways than one.

As we set out for the refugee camp, I couldn't help but look back at the house that had been our haven. It stood there, silently witnessing the stories and struggles it had sheltered within its walls. The walk to the camp was a mix of fear and an overwhelming sense of displacement. Each step away from the house was a step into the unknown, a journey of physical distance and emotional upheaval.

Arriving at the camp, we found ourselves in a sea of stories, each person and family with a journey marked by loss and survival. Once a place of learning and growth, the dormitories were now makeshift homes for refugees. As we settled into this new reality, the memory of the family who had helped us lingered like a beacon of human kindness in a world torn apart by the war.

In the camp, our days became a routine, punctuated by the ever-present hope for news of our mother. Despite the hardships, we clung to each other, finding strength in our shared resilience. Our story, a narrative of loss, survival, and the unyielding human spirit, unfolded in the heart of a city that refused to break.

******

THE DAY THE DORMS SHOOK

Once a sanctuary for students pursuing their dreams, the college dorms had become a precarious shelter under the relentless shadow of war. We knew moving there was frightening, but our options were limited. The enemy was aware that the dorms housed refugees, making it a target. Yet, in our desperate search for safety, we had nowhere else to turn. One fateful day, we found ourselves huddled in a stairwell, seeking refuge from the relentless gunfire that had become the soundtrack of our lives. My younger sister was with me, clinging close, while our other sister was on the lower floor, unaware of the horror that was about to unfold. In that moment, everything changed.

Without warning, a loud explosion tore through the air. A projectile had struck the dormitory. The world around us erupted into chaos — a vortex of dust, shattered glass, and heart-wrenching screams. My senses were overwhelmed; I couldn't hear or see. The only thing that registered was the raw panic that coursed through me. In the immediate aftermath, it was clear that the explosion had wreaked havoc. The glass wall behind us had collapsed under the force of the blast, raining down upon us. Amidst the confusion and pain, I realized with a jolt of fear that I couldn't move my leg. A sharp, searing pain told me that I had been hit in the knee.

My sister's screams pierced the chaos. The terror in her eyes was palpable as she struggled to pull me to safety. But her strength was no match for the situation we found ourselves in. As we attempted to navigate the debris-laden stairs, a horrifying sight stopped us cold, a motionless body, a student who just moments ago had been alive, now a casualty of this senseless war. As we continued our agonizing descent, my sister's cries filled the air. "Liza is dead," she kept screaming, her voice echoing with despair. The shock and confusion were overwhelming, but in this turmoil, I knew I had to act. Gathering every ounce of strength, I pulled myself up and faced her. With a firm smack, I brought her back to the present. "No, I am not dead. I am right here," I asserted, trying to anchor her and myself amid the nightmare.

That day in the dorms was a brutal reminder of the indiscriminate cruelty of war. It was a day that stripped away any remaining illusions of safety, a day that added more scars, both physical and emotional. We had survived, but at a cost that was becoming increasingly difficult to bear. As we emerged from the wreckage, the reality of our situation was evident. We were living on borrowed time; each day was a gamble against fate. Our journey, marked by constant upheaval and loss, was a relentless quest for survival in a world where peace had become a distant, and almost forgotten dream.

A FRAGILE ESCAPE

The aftermath of the explosion was a blur of urgency and pain. My younger sister and I, along with others wounded in the blast, were taken to the nearest hospital. It was a place overwhelmed by the casualties of war, where the air was thick with the scent of antiseptics and despair. As I lay on the hospital bed, I could see my sister's small frame, her body covered in dust, blood, and riddled with shrapnel particles. The sight filled me with a mixture of relief and sorrow, relief that she was alive but sorrow for the innocence that this brutal war had stolen from her. Though painful, my injury was relatively minor compared to what it could have been. A single piece of shrapnel had embedded itself in my knee, a tiny fragment of the projectile that had wreaked such havoc. The doctor, working with limited resources and no pain medication, swiftly removed it. The pain was sharp and intense, but it paled in comparison to the relief of knowing it was out. My sister received care as well. Her neck was cleaned of the shrapnel particles. Each removed piece, and the tireless efforts of the medical staff working in these impossible conditions, was a small victory.

In that hospital, surrounded by the wounded and the weary, survival was the only thing that mattered. The fact that we were still alive, still breathing, was a beacon of hope in the darkness that had surrounded our lives. Our survival that day felt like a fragile escape, a narrow miss from the clutches of death that loomed over Sarajevo.

As we left the hospital, the reality of our situation settled heavily upon us. We had survived, but so many others had not. The war continued to rage around us, each day a repeat of danger and uncertainty. But at that moment, as we stepped back into the ravaged streets, we were just grateful to be alive, to have each other, and to have the chance to see another day.

Our journey, marked by close calls and painful losses, was a constant battle to hold onto hope, to find strength in our bond, and to keep moving forward, one day at a time. In a world torn apart by conflict, these small moments of survival have kept us going, fueling our courage to persevere against all odds.

SHELTER AMONGST SOLDIERS

The room that had served as our refuge in the dorms, now in ruins, left us with yet another challenge in the relentless struggle for survival. The suggestion to use the basement as our new shelter was untenable; its use as an impromptu bathroom made it a place, we couldn't consider living in. We desperately needed a new shelter, a semblance of stability in the chaos that had become our life. In this hour of need, our brother, who had joined the army and was living in a hotel repurposed as a military base, came to our aid. His world, now intertwined with the military, vastly differed from the life we had known. The hotel, once a place of hospitality and leisure, had transformed into a shelter for soldiers, a strategic point during the war.

Reluctantly, we moved in with him, finding ourselves in an environment far removed from the civilian life we were accustomed to. The presence of armed soldiers and the constant hum of military activity were reminders of the ongoing conflict. Yet, amidst this unlikely setting, we found a surprising sense of safety and provision. The ladies in the kitchen, who managed to prepare meals even in such dire circumstances, took us under their wing. Their kindness and care were unexpected comforts, a small piece of normalcy in an otherwise turbulent existence. We were cautious, choosing to stay confined to our room, wary of the unpredictable nature of our surroundings.

Living in the hotel offered a harsh lesson: the illusion of safety behind walls was just that, an illusion. Our experience in the dorms had taught us that no place was truly safe and that the threat of projectiles loomed everywhere. Yet, in that hotel, under the protection of the army and the roof over our heads, we found a reason to be grateful. Each day was a balancing act between the fear of what lay outside our door and the gratitude for the shelter we had found. This new chapter in our journey was a constant reminder of the complexities of war where safety is a relative term, and that comfort can be found in the most unexpected places.

Our story continued to unfold in the heart of a city under siege, a narrative of adapting to ever-changing circumstances, finding fragments of hope, and clinging to each other as a war tore our world apart.

THE INCIDENT AT THE HOTEL

In the confines of that tiny room within the "military hotel" located on Marijin Dvor, my sisters and I clung to each other. We dreamt of better days and a life far removed from the horrors of war. We kept away from the windows, a precaution ingrained in us by the ever-present threat of snipers and random projectile shelling. Our world had shrunk to these four walls, a shared space that was both a sanctuary and a prison. We only ventured out of our room for meals which were served in a cafeteria downstairs. This is where we would eat alongside the soldiers. There, we encountered other girls who, like us, were navigating the treacherous terrain of life in a warzone. However, their concerns seemed distant from ours. They were there to visit brothers and boyfriends, seemingly untouched by the desperation that had become our constant companion.

One day, one of the visitors, a reckless girl, started taunting my middle sister, mocking the haircut I had given her. My sister, never one to shy away from confrontation, responded in kind. Unable to handle the retort, the girl stormed off in a huff. We thought that was the end of it, but we were wrong.

Later, as we stepped outside to enjoy a rare quiet moment free of gunfire, the same girl reappeared. Her face twisted in anger as she brandished a metal stick in her hand. It was clear she had come back for a fight. Instinctively, I told my sister to get behind me. Despite the pain in my knee, still healing from the shrapnel wound, I stood up to protect her. As the girl swung her weapon, aiming for my sister, I intercepted it. The metal hit my body, a sharp reminder of the physical pain I was already enduring. But when she raised the stick again, I struck back, driven by a primal need to defend my sister. I punched her in the face, sending her to the ground. In the heat of the moment, I found myself on top of her, continuing to defend us.

It wasn't just a fight; it was a statement. She didn't know that my sister had a protector in me, that my role had become that of a guardian, no matter the cost. As shouts erupted in the background to stop the fight, someone pulled me away, ending the altercation.

As we returned to our room that evening, the weight of what had happened sank in. Despite providing shelter, the hotel was not a place where we could find peace. The incident with the girl was a reminder that the war had seeped into every aspect of life, even into interactions that should have been mundane. I decided then, with my sisters' agreement, that it was time to find a new place to stay. We needed a space to feel safe, not just from the war outside but from the conflicts within. Our journey continued a relentless search for a haven in a city where safety was a fleeting, elusive dream.

A NEW SHELTER IN SHADOWS

Dawn brought a realization that it was time to leave the hotel, our temporary refuge among soldiers. Leaving was simple as we had nothing but the clothes on our backs. Our constant displacement had stripped us of nearly all possessions. Yet, a safer shelter was paramount, guiding us to the next refuge. We set our sights on a nearby high school in the city's quart called Drvenija, which is known to be accommodating refugees like us. Upon arrival, we inquired about a space for us to lay our heads and shield ourselves from the chaos outside. They offered us an empty classroom, a space that truly lived up to the word 'empty.' Aside from a 50-gallon barrel in the corner and a solitary gym pad on the floor, the room was bare. But to us, it was enough. In such times, expectations had to be adjusted; any roof over our heads was a luxury.

That night, as we lay on the gym pad, the cold, hard floor beneath us, we embraced this new shelter's safety. We were cold and hungry, yet there was an undeniable relief. The simplicity of the room, the starkness of our surroundings, none of it mattered. We were together, we were safe, and for that, we were profoundly grateful.

As our ritual became, we spent the night talking about the life we had left behind, about the world that had been taken from us by the war. Our conversations often circled back to our mother, her whereabouts a lingering question that haunted our every moment. "Is she looking for us?" we wondered aloud. It was a heavy burden, but in each other's company, we found the strength to keep those worries at bay, if only for a moment.

Our new home in the high school was a far cry from the life we once knew, but it was a confirmation to our adaptability and resilience. In the heart of a city torn apart by conflict, we had found yet another place to call our own, however temporary it might be. Our story, a journey marked by loss and constant movement, continued to unfold, each chapter reflecting our unyielding will to survive and keep the flicker of hope alive in the darkest times.

THE FIRE OF NECESSITY

A painful blend of emotions and harsh realities marked our first night in the empty classroom. It was a night of adapting to our circumstances and finding comfort in the smallest gestures. Most notably, it was the night I parted with the only pair of jeans I had left, the same ones I wore when we fled Foca. The classroom was bitterly cold, the cold that seeps into your bones and stays there. I remembered that I was wearing multiple layers, a small blessing that offered a bit of extra warmth. To combat the chill, we decided to start a fire. I pulled the 50-gallon barrel closer to the gym pad, our makeshift bed on the hard floor. With a heavy heart, I removed my jeans, a reminder of our home and the life we had to leave behind. Placing them into the barrel, I lit a fire.

The flames flickered to life, casting a warm, comforting glow that briefly transformed our sparse surroundings. For a moment, the warmth of the fire transported us back to our home in Foca, reminding us of a time when safety and warmth were taken for granted.

That night, as we huddled close to the fire, we found reasons to smile. There was a certain irony in burning my jeans for warmth, symbolizing how drastically our lives had changed. We lay on the gym pad, drawing close to each other to preserve the heat. Our bodies were the only barrier against the cold floor. We had nothing to cover ourselves with, no blankets or coats. Yet, in each other's presence, we found a sense of security and warmth beyond the physical. As the fire crackled beside us, we fell into a fitful sleep, our voices softly recounting stories from our childhood. These tales, filled with innocence and laughter, were a balm to our weary spirits.

That night in the classroom was not just about survival but a lesson in letting go and holding on. We let go of material possessions, understanding their insignificance in the face of our struggle to survive. But we held on to our memories, our stories, and to each other, the most precious things that no war could take away. As our journey continued each day, our resilience and bond as sisters only grew stronger.

Image created by the Author: Elizabeta Usto-Dacic

"Three Girls on a Classroom Floor"

ECHOES OF RESILIENCE

As dawn broke over Sarajevo, we awakened in our makeshift shelter within the high school's empty classroom. The morning light, filtering through the dusty windows, cast long shadows across the empty room, a visual metaphor for our current state of existence. This new day marked another chapter in our journey of survival, a continuation of our adaptation to the ever-changing landscape of a conflict-filled city.

This classroom, devoid of its traditional role as a place of learning, had become a symbol of the war's transformative impact. It was a stark reminder of how the familiar can be repurposed in times of need and how spaces meant for growth and knowledge were now shelters for the displaced. Despite the spartan conditions, we found solace in its relative safety and the privacy it afforded us, a rare luxury in our current nomadic life.

Our days in high school were a blend of monotonous routine and anxious anticipation. Each morning, we would scour the building for resources: a few scraps of food, water, anything that could ease our daily struggle. The school, once buzzing with the chatter and energy of students, now echoed with the sounds of refugees, each carrying their own story of loss and survival. We filled our time with moments of deep reflection. The empty classroom walls became the canvas for our thoughts, where memories of our past life in Foca and our aspirations for the future mingled. These reflective moments were crucial, as they allowed us to process our experiences, grieve for what we had lost, and find strength in our shared journey. The war had stripped us of our material possessions, but it had also honed our ability to find joy and meaning in the simplest things: a shared laugh, a moment of quiet contemplation, and the comforting presence of each other.

In the evenings, we would gather around our small fire, the flames casting a warm, flickering light that pushed back the room's chill. These moments around the fire were more than just a means to stay warm; they were a time for us to reconnect, share stories and dreams, and maintain a sense of normalcy in a world that had turned upside down. During these gatherings, we realized that hope became a survival tool, a beacon guiding us through the darkest times.

The high school, with its empty classrooms and long hallways, also became a place of unexpected learning. We learned about resilience, the strength of the human spirit, and the power of hope. We discovered the profound impact of empathy and kindness, often from fellow refugees and sometimes from the residents who would occasionally bring food or supplies.

As we navigated our days in this new shelter, we were constantly reminded of the broader context of the war. The distant sounds of artillery shells, the sporadic gunfire, and the ever-present sense of danger served as a backdrop to our daily existence. These sounds, though frightening, also deepened our understanding of the conflict, its complexities, and its impact on the people of Sarajevo and beyond.

Our stay in the high school was a chapter characterized by a duality of experiences: the harsh realities of war compared with the enduring human capacity for adaptation and resilience. It was a time of personal growth, deepening bonds, and an unwavering commitment to hope, even in the face of overwhelming dangers. This chapter of our story, set in the shadows of a war-torn city, highlighted the unyielding spirit of survival and the unbreakable bond of sisterhood that sustained us through one of the most challenging periods of our lives.

THE NIGHT OF TERROR

The memory of that night is etched in my mind with a clarity that time has not dimmed. The darkness of the classroom, our temporary refuge, was abruptly shattered by a knock on the door. Hope surged within me, a fleeting thought that it could be my brother coming with food or news. But the reality that unfolded was far from what I had imagined. As I opened the door, the sharp, unexpected pain of a punch sent me reeling backward, my body sliding across the cold floor. The attacker, a man consumed by rage, quickly turned his fury towards my middle sister, striking her with such force that she was left trembling and sick. The room, once a haven, had transformed into a horror scene. My youngest sister's screams pierced the air, a sound that resonated with my fear and shock.

Lying on the floor, dazed and in pain, I saw the man looming over me. His anger was palpable, his kicks hitting my body with a brutality that seemed to know no bounds. Then, in a moment that felt like an eternity, he drew a gun, pointing it directly at my face. My mind raced, fear and defiance intertwining. The thought that the enemy was capturing us and that our haven had been breached filled me with a dread so profound that death seemed a preferable fate. I yelled at him, challenging him to shoot, as I yelled:" shoot," preferring death over the terror of captivity.

The commotion had drawn attention. People from other classrooms began intervening, awakened by the screams and commotion. Their voices, filled with confusion and anger, demanded to know the reason behind this senseless violence. The man's rationale was unknown to me, his actions seemingly fueled by a deep-seated anger that defied understanding.

As he retreated from the classroom, his parting words were a chilling threat, promising death if he found us there again. The door closed behind him, leaving us in shock and disbelief. The sanctity of our shelter had been violated; the illusion of safety was brutally shattered. We were left to process the terror of the encounter, the physical pain of the assault, and the deep psychological scars it inflicted.

The incident was a warning, a reminder of life's unpredictable and volatile nature in a war-torn city. The ever-present danger was not just from the conflict outside but also from the individuals within, whose actions could be driven by fear, anger, or desperation. That night, we faced the external threats of war and the internal threat posed by those who, like us, were caught in the vortex of conflict. This chapter of our story was one of the darkest, a night when the fragility of our existence was laid bare. It underscored the harsh reality that the line between friend and foe can blur in times of war, and violence can emerge from the most unexpected places. The experience left an indelible mark on us and a reminder of the need to be vigilant, to protect each other, and to navigate the unpredictable landscape of a city under siege.

Our road to freedom continued. With each step forward, our ability to withstand war trials and the determination to survive never wavered. Despite the terror of that night, our spirits, though bruised, remained unbroken, driven by the hope of better days and the unshakable bond that united us as sisters.

VIGILANCE IN THE SHADOWS

The day after the assault, a resolve stronger than fear took root within me. Armed with a small axe borrowed from a friend, I stationed myself by the door, determined to protect my sisters at all costs. The echo of the previous night's terror still lingered, but it had transformed into a steely determination. I was no longer just a victim of circumstances; I had become a guardian, a role I embraced with fierce protectiveness.

As I waited, the hours stretched, each minute a test of patience and vigilance. The man never returned, but my readiness to defend us never wavered. This readiness was not born from a desire for violence but from a deep-seated need to ensure the safety of my siblings. In those moments, I realized the extent of my strength and the lengths I would go to shield my family from harm. I was not scared of him. Outside, the streets of Sarajevo were the epicenter of the more significant conflict. Snipers, hidden in their cowardly perches, targeted innocent civilians, their bullets a cruel reminder of the senselessness of this war. The indiscriminate shelling, the "pressing of buttons" that sent projectiles tearing through the city, was a confirmation of the cowardice of those who waged war from a distance, detached from the human cost of their actions. Those were the "people" that I feared.

As I reflected on this, a profound anger and sorrow filled me. The faceless enemies, those who targeted us from afar, represented the worst of humanity. Their actions, devoid of honor or courage, stood in stark contrast to the bravery shown by the ordinary people of Sarajevo, who faced each day with a resilience that was nothing short of heroic.

In that cold classroom, with the axe by my side, I pondered the depths of human cruelty and the remarkable capacity for endurance. This war had stripped us of so much, yet it had also revealed the strength of the human spirit. Amidst the fear and uncertainty, a sense of solidarity bound us all, a shared determination to survive the horrors that besieged us.

As I sat with my sisters that evening, I shared my thoughts. I spoke of the courage it takes to stand up against injustice, the importance of defending oneself, and the values this conflict ingrained in us. This war, in all its brutality, was also a teacher. It taught us about the fragility of life, the importance of standing up for what is right, and the power of hope in the darkest of times.

Our conversation shifted deep into the history of our region, the complex tapestry of cultures and ethnicities that had coexisted for centuries. I explained how the war had its roots in a tangled web of political ambitions and historical grievances and how it manifested deeper issues that had simmered for generations. As we talked, I emphasized the importance of understanding our past and recognizing the lessons that our history offers. This understanding was crucial for making sense of the present conflict and shaping a future where such atrocities would never be repeated. Our cultural heritage, with its rich traditions and diverse influences, was a beacon that guided us through these tumultuous times.

As we lay in the quiet classroom that night, a sense of cautious hope surrounded us. Our challenges were daunting, but we were no longer passive observers of our fate. We had become active participants in our survival, armed with the knowledge of our past and the unwavering resolve to forge a better future. The chapter closed with us falling asleep, the axe still by the door, symbolizing our readiness to face whatever challenges lay ahead. Our journey was far from over, but we were moving forward with a newfound strength and a deep understanding of the resilience that defined us.

THE STRUGGLE FOR EXISTENCE

In the heart of Sarajevo, besieged and battered by the war, food became a luxury few could afford. The city, once thriving with markets and cafes, now bore the scars of conflict, its shelves empty and its streets filled with the hunger of its people. For my sisters and me, survival hinged on the meager rations provided by the public soup kitchen, a lifeline in these desperate times.

The portions they handed out resembled a meal and were more valuable than any delicacy we had known in our "previous" life. Accompanied by a quarter loaf of bread, these rations were our only source of sustenance. The bread symbolized happiness, a small but significant reminder of normalcy in a world turned upside down.

As the days melded into a monotonous cycle of queuing for food and retreating to our cold classroom, I realized that waiting was not enough. A gnawing sense of urgency took hold of me – a need to act, to change our fate. I knew we couldn't continue like this indefinitely. I had to find a way to get us out of the city, out of this siege that was slowly choking the life out of us. But this task, this thought of escaping Sarajevo, loomed as my greatest challenge. We needed more money, resources, and a clear plan. The city surrounded, its exits guarded, its freedom stripped away by the war. Yet, despite these daunting obstacles, the drive to reunite with our mother and to find safety for my sisters fueled my determination.

We only had each other and the dream of finding our mom. That dream became our beacon, guiding us through the darkest days. It reminded us of what we were fighting for – not just survival, but the hope of a reunion, of rebuilding the family that war had torn apart.

In a city under siege, where each day was a battle against despair, I began to forge a plan. I didn't know how or when, but I was ready to find a way out for us. Our story, a witness of the power of hope and the strength of familial bonds, was far from over. The road ahead was unclear, but the possibility of a future beyond the war's shadows spurred me on.

THE CROSSROADS OF DECISION

Time marked by days and the places we sought refuge in the relentless continuum of the war. We moved from one shelter to another, each step a calculated move closer to the other side of Sarajevo. This plan was a desperate strategy for escape, for a chance at a life beyond the ceaseless bombardment and the pervasive shadow of death.

I found a glimmer of hope through a government agency, a pathway out of the chaos. I applied and, against all odds, received documents that allowed us to leave the country. Being children without parents, without permanent shelter, and with our place of birth being Vienna, Austria, we received permission to join a refugee convoy. This convoy, filled with women and children, was our ticket to a new beginning, a chance to rebuild what the war had shattered.

As I held the documents, the reality of our situation hit me with a force. I wasn't ready for that. My emotions were a tumultuous sea, waves of relief and guilt crashing against each other. On one hand, there was the relief of knowing that my sisters and I had a chance to escape, to find safety. On the other, there was an unbearable guilt: the thought of leaving without knowing where our mother was, without paying respects at the graves of our brothers. These thoughts haunted me, a relentless echo in my mind: "How could we leave our mother behind? How could we turn our backs on the city that had been our home, on the memories of our brothers who had perished in this war?" The thought of stepping onto that bus and driving away from Sarajevo was as painful as any physical wound I had endured. This internal struggle, this clash of survival instinct and familial bonds, ultimately made our decision. We chose to stay. The determination to find our mother and survive the war outweighed the promise of safety. It was a decision that came with its risks and its own set of fears, but it was one we needed to make.

In the heart of a city still gripped by conflict, we found a new kind of strength: the strength to face the unknown, to hold onto hope when it seemed futile. Our journey was far from over, but our resolve to stand together as a family to face the days ahead remained unshaken. The war had taken much from us, but it had not taken our spirit, our unwavering commitment to each other, and the memory of the brothers we had lost.

******

UNEXPECTED KINSHIPIN DEVASTATION

Our journey to the other side of Sarajevo unfolded with an unexpected turn. In a city torn apart by war, we stumbled upon a fragment of our past: families from our hometown, Foca. These people, once just familiar faces, and neighbors, transformed into our closest kin in this time of shared adversity. Their homes, though temporary and borne out of necessity, became havens for us, where we found shelter and a sense of belonging.

The generosity we encountered was humbling. These families, grappling with their struggles, opened their doors to us. They shared their food, which was scarce; they offered us clothes, a luxury in times like these; and most importantly, they provided a place to sleep, a respite from the relentless unpredictability that had become our daily life. Word of our family's tragedy had somehow preceded us.

They knew of the loss of our brothers, a sorrow that hung silently between us, a shared understanding of pain and loss. Yet, despite this knowledge, they were unaware of our mother's whereabouts. This gap in our story added to the weight I carried each day, the weight of not knowing, of yearning for a reunion that seemed increasingly elusive.

Amidst these newfound family members' kindness and support, my days were filled with sadness and a deep sense of helplessness. The longing to know my mother's fate and ensure my sisters' safety consumed me. I was caught in limbo, torn between the safety and solidarity we had found here, and the gnawing need to move forward, to break free from the constraints of the besieged city.

The decision to leave Sarajevo was not just about seeking physical safety. This was also an attempt to reclaim some control over our lives, to break away from the helplessness that had enveloped us. With all its memories and scars, the city had become a labyrinth of sorrow from which we needed to escape. The resolve solidified within me as I lay awake at night, listening to the distant echoes of artillery fire. We had to leave. The path ahead was fraught with unknowns, but the drive to find our mother, to rebuild our shattered lives, was a force stronger than fear. Our journey continued to wind its way through the landscapes of war, each step a movement towards hope and a future we yearned to reclaim.

******

THE LEAP OF FAITH

The winter of 1993 in Sarajevo was as bleak and unforgiving as the year that preceded it, a relentless cold that seeped into our bones and our spirits. Yet, amid this frigid despair, a flicker of hope arrived with my middle brother. He brought news about our mother, which cut through the fog of our daily survival. He had heard that she had escaped the besieged city of Gorazde and had reached a village near Sarajevo.

Initially, I was skeptical of his news, suspecting it might be a well-intentioned ruse to encourage us to leave the city. But as he spoke, the earnestness in his eyes and the detail in his words began to chip away at my disbelief. The thought that our mother was so close, yet still so far, reignited a sense of urgency within me, a desperate need to reunite with her. The plan to leave Sarajevo was fraught with peril. The only viable escape route was a daunting sprint across the airport runway, an expanse constantly under the watch of snipers and artillery fire. It was a risk that could easily cost us our lives, yet the possibility of seeing our mother again, of reuniting our fractured family, pushed us to take this gamble.

In the whirlwind of preparing, a stark realization dawned upon us – we only had two pairs of shoes among the three of us. The decision of who would go and who would stay was heart-wrenching. My youngest sister, barely 13, had grown increasingly attached to me, her fear and hesitancy mirrored in her eyes. My middle sister, ever the pragmatic one, proposed that she stay behind, allowing me and our youngest sister to make the difficult, and dangerous journey. The weight of this decision was immense. To leave my middle sister behind was unthinkable, yet the necessity of the situation demanded such sacrifices. It was a choice no one should ever have to make: deciding between the safety of one sibling and the potential reunion with a lost parent.

That night, as we huddled together, the reality of our situation surrounded us. We were about to embark on a journey that could lead us to our mother or into the arms of death. But the chance, however slim, of reuniting our family was a chance we had to take.

The following day, with a heavy heart and in the middle of the night, we made our way to the edge of the airport. It was a moment of truth, a leap of faith into the unknown, driven by love, hope, and the unbreakable bond of family. Our story, a journey marked by loss, resilience, and the relentless pursuit of reunion, was taking another critical turn.

THE HARROWING CROSSING

The night we decided to leave Sarajevo was shrouded in a tense, eerie silence, starkly contrasting the constant din of war that had become our norm. It was time to make our perilous journey across the airport runway, a daunting expanse between us and the hope of finding our mother. My sister, the one I had to leave behind, watched with a brave face, her eyes glistening with unshed tears.

As I exited the building, the cold night air hit me with its biting chill. My brother was waiting for me, but he was not alone. A group of young, Bosnian soldiers, his friends, had come to aid us in our daring escape. They were armed, a necessary precaution in a city where danger lurked at every corner.

Approaching the airport, the reality of what we were about to do sank in. The runway stretched beyond us, vast and intimidating under the starlit sky. The snow, untouched and deep, blanketed the ground, reaching up to my waist. It was an obstacle I hadn't anticipated, adding another layer of difficulty to our dangerous escape.

As we started our crossing, I quickly realized that running was impossible. The depth of the snow, combined with my lingering knee injury, made every step a struggle. I fell repeatedly, each time feeling more helpless and frightened. But the soldiers, true to their word of assistance, were there to help, pulling me up and supporting me through the treacherous snow. Our progress could have been faster, hindered by the need to stop and cut through wires that crisscrossed the field, remnants of the war's attempts to cordon off and control every inch of the city. With every pause, I braced myself for the sound of gunfire, for the burst of a flare that would expose us to the enemy. But miraculously, the night remained quiet. It was as if the war had decided to hold its breath, granting us a brief respite.

That night's silence was uncanny, almost surreal. The usual soundtrack of conflict was absent, replaced by the muffled sounds of our movement through the snow and the occasional snip of wire cutters. It was a silence that heightened our senses, a tense calm that made the possibility of sudden violence more jarring.

Reaching the other side of the airport felt like emerging from a nightmare into an uncertain dawn. We had made it through one of the most dangerous parts of our journey, aided by the bravery and kindness of Bosnian soldiers who saw our struggle and chose to help.

That cold, quiet night was a turning point in our journey. It was a confirmation that unexpected moments of humanity and solidarity can arise even during war. It was a night that brought us one step closer to our mother, to the reunion we longed for, and a step further from the city that had been both our home and our prison. Our story, etched with the scars of war and the resilience of the human spirit, continued to unfold under the starlit sky of Sarajevo.

******

THE ROAD OVER MOUNT IGMAN

The successful crossing of the airport runway was a triumph, but it marked only the beginning of our journey to find our mother. Ahead of us lay Mount Igman, a mountain that once symbolized leisure and beauty, known for its ski slopes and vacation spots. Now, it stood as a formidable barrier on our path to freedom.

The night was deep and cold, the kind of cold that seeps into your bones and saps your strength. But there was no time for rest; our journey had to continue. We embarked on the trek across Mount Igman, navigating through dirt roads, hiking paths, and dense forests. The terrain was rough, and the snow-covered paths were treacherous underfoot, but our determination kept us moving forward.

The journey across the mountain was grueling, stretching throughout the night, and for hours. Our progress was slow as each step was a battle against fatigue and the biting cold. As dawn began to break, painting the sky with the first light of the new day, we approached a small village, a cluster of just a few houses in the embrace of the mountain.

Hunger gnawed at us with relentless intensity. Seeing a man emerge from one of the houses, I gathered the courage to approach him and ask for a piece of bread. The man, after a brief pause, told us to wait. Moments later, he returned with a generous piece of homemade bread. It was more than just food; it was a gesture of kindness that touched our weary hearts. We thanked him profusely, my sister and I splitting the bread as we continued our journey, savoring each bite.

Our brother, our steadfast guide through this ordeal, kept a brisk pace, his focus unwavering. We often asked him: "How much longer?" His response was always the same: "One more hour." But the hours stretched into another full day of walking and then into the evening. The journey over Mount Igman was more than a physical challenge; it tested our mental and emotional endurance. Each step took us further away from the war-torn city we had known and closer to the hope of reuniting with our mother. Despite the exhaustion and the hunger, we pushed forward, driven by the unyielding spirit that had carried us this far.

Our journey, even in the face of overwhelming odds, continued to unfold with each step we took. The mountain, once a symbol of leisure and joy, had become a part of our arduous journey, a bridge between the life we had left behind and the future we were striving to reach.

THE THRESHOLD OF REUNION

After the seemingly endless trek, the cover of the night found us arriving at a small, secluded village. The scene was far different from a war-torn Sarajevo we had left behind. Here, the houses were dimly lit by the gentle glow of candlelight, casting soft shadows that danced against the walls. My heart was heavy with anticipation and a tinge of skepticism as my brother confidently declared our arrival. In my mind, doubts whirled. "How can he be certain which house it is?" I wondered silently.

He led us to the first house nestled under a massive bridge, an unassuming structure that held the potential to end our long search. With a mixture of hope and apprehension, we knocked on the door. When it creaked open, revealing a stranger, I took a deep breath and spoke. "I am looking for my mom, Semsa," I said, my voice barely above a whisper, laden with the weight of our journey.

What happened next felt like a dream. The woman's eyes widened with recognition, and she quickly responded, "She is next door, at the neighbor's house. I will run to get her." Her voice had an unmistakable excitement, a shared joy in the imminent reunion. She ushered us inside, her eagerness to assist palpable.

We stepped into the warmth of the house, each of us processing the moment in our way. The possibility that we might finally see our mother again after all this time, after all the miles and the hardships, was overwhelming. The wait, even just those few minutes as the lady hurried to fetch our mother, felt like an eternity. The room was filled with a tense, expectant silence. My sister and I exchanged glances, a whirlwind of emotions reflected in our eyes – hope, fear, longing. The lady's quick departure confirmed that we had come to the right place and our journey was reaching its crescendo.

Then, there were footsteps, a sound growing louder and more distinct. The anticipation in the room rose to an almost unbearable level. We stood there, united by our shared ordeal, on the precipice of a moment that would redefine our lives. The door opened, and time seemed to stand still. In the doorway stood our mother, a figure we had longed to see for what felt like a lifetime. The reunion and the end of our search were finally at hand. It was a moment of unbridled emotion, culminating our journey through the heart of war. This night marked our enduring family bond in the face of unimaginable trials.

******

ECHOES OF JOY AND SORROW

In that small, candle-lit room, time froze as we stood face-to-face with our mother. The reunion was a whirlwind of emotions, a blend of immense joy and profound sorrow. Our mother, once familiar, now bore the marks of the war's toll on her. Her eyes, small and sunken, were pools of sadness; her face, aged beyond the years that had passed; her body, a reflection of the hardship she had endured, thin and weary. Yet, amidst these changes, her voice rang clear and true – it was hers.

Tears flowed freely in the room, not just from us but from the kind lady and her children, who had been stirred from their sleep by the noise. They watched, wide-eyed, as our family, torn apart by war, came together in a bittersweet reunion.

My mother's reaction was heart-wrenching. Overcome with emotion, she wept loudly, repeating, "It's true, Liza is dead." The shock and grief had blurred her recognition; she couldn't see that I was standing right there, alive and in front of her. "No, it's me. I am right here," I kept saying, trying to break through the veil of her disbelief as she couldn't recognize me. There was a palpable absence during our reunion, my sister, who had stayed behind. I quickly explained to our mother the heartbreaking decision we had to make, that we didn't have enough shoes for all of us to undertake the journey. I assured her that our brother would return to bring her to us soon. It was a promise that brought a flicker of relief to her eyes, a hope amid the chaos.

In that humble village home, we held each other tightly, the pieces of our fragmented family coming together once more. The room was filled with the sounds of our reunion: cries, laughter, and the murmurs of a family reweaving the bonds stretched across time and distance. Our journey, marked by loss, resilience, and an unwavering will to find each other, had led us to this moment. Against all odds, we had reunited with our mother, a beacon of hope in the relentless darkness of war. Our story had reached a pivotal chapter of reunion and healing, and we were looking forward to the day when our family would be together again.

******

A NIGHT OF WARMTH AND REUNION

The night of our reunion with our mother was filled with an energy and warmth that had been missing from our lives for far too long. Her excitement was palpable as she bustled around the room, her movements quick and purposeful, driven by a mother's instinct to care for her children. She wrapped us in whatever covers she could find, her words a soft murmur under her breath, "They are alive." It was a relief mantra, a mother's most profound fears laid to rest.

As the night wore on, the adrenaline that had fueled us began to wane, giving way to an overwhelming sense of exhaustion. The journey from Sarajevo, though successful, had drained us physically and emotionally. Despite the lack of beds in the house, the floor became our resting place. It was a familiar situation for my sister and me, reminiscent of the nights spent on the cold, hard classroom floor. But this time, it was different: the room was warm, filled with the presence of our mother, a comfort we hadn't realized how much we had missed.

Lying there, I couldn't bring myself to ask our mother about our brothers. The joy of our reunion seemed too precious, too fragile to risk with painful questions. She was basking in the relief of seeing us alive, and I couldn't bear to dim the light of her happiness with the shadow of our loss.

In hushed tones, we recounted our journey from Sarajevo, sharing details of the harrowing escape and the people who had helped us along the way. Our voices were low, and as we talked, the weariness of our bodies and the comfort of being together, safe, and warm, lulled us into sleep. That night, as we drifted off just before dawn, there was a sense of peace, a feeling that, for the moment, all was right in our world. Our reunion with our mother was a beacon of hope, a reminder that there are moments of joy and relief even in the dark times. Our story, a tapestry woven with the threads of war, loss, and survival, had found a spot of light in the enduring love of a reunited family.

A MORNING OF PEACE

The morning after our reunion was a new beginning in more ways than one. Waking up early, still adjusting to the reality that we were finally with our mother, I stepped outside to take in our surroundings. The contrast between here and Sarajevo was stark and almost disorienting. There was a sense of peace, an absence of the gunfire and chaos that had become the soundtrack of our lives in the city. It was a tranquility that felt both surreal and desperately welcome.

As I looked around, one of the first things that caught my eye was a natural water source. It was such a simple, everyday sight, yet it held a significance I couldn't have imagined just a short while ago. Having not seen running water for almost two years, the sight of it was strangely moving. It reminded me of all the essential comforts of life that the war had stripped away from us.

My mom joined me outside, her presence comforting in this new and unfamiliar place. She explained that most people living in these houses were, like us, refugees from our hometown of Foca. Each family, each person, carried their story of displacement, their burden of loss. They, too, were searching for their loved ones, holding onto hope for reunions amidst the skepticism and upheaval of war.

This village, a gathering place for scattered souls, was a community of an immense tragedy unfolding across our country. It was a refuge for those uprooted by conflict, a temporary haven where life continued in the shadow of war. Here, amidst fellow refugees, there was a shared understanding, an unspoken bond forged by everyday experiences and shared losses.

As I stood there, taking in the peaceful morning, the well, and the houses around us, I reflected on our journey. We had traversed a path fraught with danger to find our mother and this semblance of peace. The war continued to rage just miles away, yet here, in this small village, we found a momentary escape from its grasp. Our story, intertwined with the stories of so many others displaced by the war, was a testimony to the enduring human spirit, to the resilience that keeps us moving forward in the face of overwhelming odds. The village, with its natural well and houses filled with refugees, was not just a place on a map but a symbol of hope. A symbol of the enduring quest for reunion and peace.

RETURN TO UNCERTAINTY

As winter's grip loosened and the ground thawed, we faced the changing seasons with hope. Our small family had reunited. Our sister had joined us, brought over by our brother through the same difficult journey we had undertaken. For a moment, we embraced the joy of being together again.

In front of the house, we took advantage of the fertile soil, planting potatoes in a small patch of land. In a time when food was a scarce and precious commodity, the ability to grow even a modest crop felt like a luxury. The potatoes symbolized more than sustenance; they were a sign of hope, a small assertion of control over our lives in a world where so much was unreliable. But this period of relative calm and hope was short-lived. The harsh reality of war soon intruded upon our fragile peace. News arrived that the enemy forces were advancing, their approach marked by the intensifying sound of gunfire and the devastating aftermath they left in their wake. Villages are ravaged, and their inhabitants faced unspeakable horrors. We decided to evacuate the village. Our options were limited, the only direction was back to Sarajevo. The city we had fled, which we had risked so much to escape, was our sole refuge.

The decision to return was heavy with a sense of defeat and apprehension. Still embroiled in conflict, Sarajevo offered no promise of safety or stability. Yet, it was a choice made of necessity, a move dictated by the ruthless progression of the war. As we prepared to leave the village, the brief relative peace we had enjoyed seemed like a distant memory. The garden we had tended, the small joys of family reunification, were overshadowed by the looming threat of violence. Our journey back to Sarajevo was a return to uncertainty, to the familiar landscape of danger and survival.

Our story, a narrative woven through with the threads of war, resilience, and the unyielding human spirit, continued. Each step back towards the city was a step into the unknown, witnessing our determination to endure and to hold onto hope in this chaos.

THE COURAGEOUS RETURN

Standing on the edge of the airport runway, the tranquility of the village we had briefly called home felt like a world away. The reality of our situation hit us with full force. We were about to make the dangerous dash across the airport again, but our mother was with us this time, leading the way. There were others with us, on our desperate journey. Alongside us were other women, each with their own stories of loss and survival, clutching their children's hands tightly. The air was thick with tension, the collective anxiety of the group palpable as we prepared for the risky crossing under the cover of night.

As we waited for the right moment to run, my mother's voice cut through the darkness, giving us instructions on what to do and, crucially, what not to do. As I gazed at her in the dim light, all I could see was her extraordinary bravery. A sense of awe washed over me. "She is so strong, so brave," I thought. In that moment, she was more than just our mother, she was our hero. Despite the unimaginable pain of losing two sons, her resolve to ensure our safety remained unshaken. Her strength was our guiding light.

Then came the signal. It was time. We grabbed each other's hands, forming a chain bound by love and necessity. And with that, we began our dash across the open runway. With its familiar yet scarred skyline, the city of Sarajevo lay ahead, drawing us back to its embrace.
Our determination, and the hurried steps on the tarmac, echoed in the silent night. Each step was a defiance of the war that sought to claim us, a physical manifestation of our will to survive and protect each other. Our mother's figure was a beacon of courage in the surrounding darkness, leading us unflinchingly across the danger.

As we ran, with the lights of Sarajevo growing closer, there was a profound understanding that there was no turning back. Our journey, fraught with trials and marked by both loss and resilience, continued to push us forward. In the chaos, our family's unbreakable bond and our mother's unwavering courage were our sources of strength, guiding us through the darkness toward the hope of a safer tomorrow.

THE PERILOUS RETURN

The sprint across the airport runway was full of fear and unpredictability. With every step, we were aware that, at any moment, enemy gunfire could erupt, turning our dash for freedom into a deadly trap. The danger was not just from the enemy, we also had to evade the United Nations peacekeeping trucks patrolling the area. Their role was to maintain peace, but for us, they represented another threat: if caught, they would send us back to the start, undoing our difficult journey.

The run felt endless, a grueling endurance test under the most harrowing circumstances. My sisters, my mother, and I pushed our bodies beyond exhaustion, driven by the sheer will to survive. Finally, when we couldn't run any further, we crossed. The relief of crossing the airport was mixed with a heavy dread. Returning to Sarajevo was not a cause for celebration. Still, in the throes of war, the city offered no respite from the turmoil we had momentarily escaped. Sarajevo, once our home, now stood as a symbol of despair. The lack of electricity, water, and food; the ever-present threat of projectiles and gunfire; the snipers lying in wait to claim their next victim, all these elements painted a grim picture of our daily reality. Who would choose to be in a place where every step could be your last?

Despite the overwhelming challenges, there was a flicker of hope in the fact that we were together. Our family's unity was the one constant in a world turned upside down. The thread held us together, giving us the strength to face each new day in this war-torn city. I clung to the belief that this war would eventually end. The hope for peace and a day when we could live without fear was a distant dream, but it was a dream that kept us going. Our story, a narrative of survival against all odds, continued amidst a city fighting for its soul. The hope we held onto was not just for our safety but for the restoration of our home, for a future where Sarajevo could once again be a place of life, not just survival.

A BITTERSWEET ARRIVAL

Under the luminous glow of a moonlit sky, we reached the other side of the airport runway, a feat that seemed almost miraculous in its execution. The adrenaline that had propelled us across the expanse continued to pulse through our veins, a frenetic energy that was part relief, part unresolved tension. The experience was intense and indescribable: a mixture of fear, determination, and the sheer will to survive.

As we paused, catching our breaths, the reality of our situation began to sink in. The relief of having made it across alive was tempered by the recognition of what lay ahead. Sarajevo, our destination, was no sanctuary. The notion of freedom, which had seemed so close as we ran under the cover of night, dissipated as we faced the city's grim reality. Still, in the grip of war, Sarajevo offered no respite from the conflict that had driven us away. The familiar sounds of gunfire and exploding projectiles welcomed us back, a grim reminder of the city's ongoing strife. The scarcity of water and food and the omnipresent danger of death were challenges we had hoped to leave behind but found waiting for us.

With no shelter to return to, our arrival in Sarajevo was marked not by a sense of homecoming but by a renewed sense of riskiness. The city, battered and bruised by the war, was far from what we once knew. It was a harsh reminder that our journey was far from over.

As we stood amidst the ruins of our once-beloved city, we faced a critical question: where do we go from here? The roads stretching before us were as unclear as the paths we had already traversed. But one thing was clear: we refused to give up. Our resilience, tested time and again, remained unbroken. The road back to where we started was not just a physical journey but a symbol of our enduring spirit and refusal to succumb to despair. The chronicles of our survival against overwhelming odds continued in the streets of Sarajevo. Each step forward gave us the strength to keep moving, to find a way through the chaos, and towards a future where peace and safety were more than just distant dreams.

A NEW SHELTER IN THE SHADOWS

In the depths of the night, with our mother now by our side, we navigated Sarajevo's familiar yet hauntingly empty streets to the only refuge we knew: the home of our neighbors who had become like family. They had previously opened their doors to my sisters and me when we had nowhere else to turn, and now they welcomed us again, this time with our mother in tow. The reunion was bittersweet, and the night was spent in a collective embrace of shared stories and experiences. We huddled in the darkness, conserving the precious candlelight, each narrative weaving a tapestry of resilience and survival. The room was filled with the soft murmurs of our voices, recounting the ordeals we had faced and the journey that had brought us back to Sarajevo.

During our conversations, our temporary hosts proposed an idea that offered a glimmer of hope in our dire situation. They suggested we find an empty apartment close by and make it our temporary shelter. The concept was born out of necessity, a common practice in a town where the standard rules of society had been upended by war. Many fled their homes, leaving empty spaces that had become makeshift refuges for those displaced by the conflict. The idea of breaking into an apartment reminded us of the desperate times we were living in. It was a plan born out of survival, not desire. The notion of taking over an abandoned space was a moral dilemma, but survival often meant making difficult choices in a city besieged by war.

The following morning, armed with this plan, we set out to find a place we could temporarily call our own. The streets of Sarajevo, scarred by the ongoing conflict, were a labyrinth of lost homes and dreams. Our search was not just for a physical space but for a semblance of stability, a place where we could gather our strength and continue to face the challenges ahead. Our journey, marked by unending trials and an unbreakable family bond, continued in the war-torn landscape of Sarajevo. Each step was a witness to our resilience, our ability to adapt and survive in the face of overwhelming adversity. The search for a temporary shelter was more than just a quest for a roof over our heads. It was a search for a fleeting sense of normalcy in a world turned upside down.

A NEW CHAPTER IN THE STUDIO APARTMENT

After much searching, our journey led us to a small studio apartment on the ground level of a nondescript building. It was empty, a hollow shell void of the warmth and life it once held. The cold, bare walls echoed the desolation of the city outside, yet to us, it represented a newfound refuge, a place to anchor ourselves amid the turmoil. This modest studio apartment, with its unassuming façade, was set to become the backdrop of a significant chapter in our lives. Here, we would form bonds of friendship and love, where we would experience the complexities of human relationships amidst the stark realities of war. In this confined space, we would witness the blend of good and evil that life often presents, especially in conflict. The apartment, with its limited space, forced us to adapt and find comfort in the simplicity of our surroundings. It became our haven, where we could momentarily escape the harshness of the war outside. The walls of the studio, which initially seemed cold and unwelcoming, gradually absorbed the essence of our presence, transforming into a home filled with our hopes, fears, and dreams.

As the days turned into weeks and months, the studio apartment witnessed the changes in our lives. It was a place of laughter, tears, whispered secrets, and shared dreams. Within its confines, we experienced the tumultuous emotions of adolescence: the excitement of first loves, the heartache of partings, and the deep bonds of friendship forged in adversity. Yet, there were times of difficulty and challenge alongside these moments of joy and growth. The ever-present war continued to cast its shadow over our lives, a constant reminder of the uncertainty ahead.

Our experiences in the apartment mirrored the complexities of life during wartime and moments of happiness interwoven with times of hardship. In this small studio apartment, our lives unfolded in unexpected ways. Destiny had led us to this place, where each day was a lesson in resilience, in making the most of what we had. Our story, set against the backdrop of a city fighting for survival, is a witness to the adaptability and the enduring strength of the human spirit. Here, in this unassuming space, we continued to live, love, and hope, embracing the changes that life brought, the good and the bad.

AN UNEXPECTED ENCOUNTER

My middle sister, embracing a spirit of service amidst the chaos, had begun volunteering with the Red Cross. One day, she returned to our studio apartment but wasn't alone. From under our window, I heard her call my name, "Liza." Curious, I peered through the window and saw her standing there with someone. When I inquired about her companion, she excitedly told me he was a friend she wanted me to meet. My response was immediate and dismissive: "No way, I am not interested." The truth was what I saw didn't pique my interest. He was a tall, skinny guy with shoulder-length hair in a ripped, dirty army uniform. He tried to be humorous, calling me to come outside, but I wasn't amused. I closed the window, uninterested in this stranger.

Despite my apparent lack of interest, he persisted. He would come under my window every day, calling out my name to catch my attention. I would pretend not to be home, avoiding any interaction. My mom, ever the voice of reason, cautioned me not to be mean. "He likes you," she would say, encouraging me to be friendly and meet him. "You never know," she added, suggesting that there might be something more worth exploring. Reluctantly, I eventually gave in to my mom's and sister's persistence. I stepped outside to meet him, unaware that this simple act would alter the course of my life. It was a meeting that, at the time, seemed inconsequential, yet it marked the beginning of a journey that would intertwine our lives in ways I could never have imagined.

This unexpected encounter, which started with skepticism and reluctance, soon unfolded into something more profound. Amidst the backdrop of war and the struggle for survival, a new relationship began to blossom. It was a relationship that brought hope and a touch of normalcy in an otherwise turbulent world. Our story, woven through life's challenges in a war-torn city, was taking another turn.

This chance meeting under my window was not just about finding love. It was a reminder that even in the darkest times, life continues in all its complexity, bringing new connections, new beginnings, and unforeseen changes.

THE BLOSSOMING OF AN UNLIKELY LOVE

At first, our interactions were awkward, laden with the discomfort of two strangers attempting to bridge two very different worlds. He, a soldier weathered by the harsh realities of war, and I, a young woman, tried to find a sense of normalcy amidst the chaos. Our conversations started stilted, filled with mundane topics. But as days turned into weeks, a comfortable rhythm developed between us. He often shared stories of his life before the war: tales of childhood, childhood dreams, and the places he wished to see. I was drawn to his resilience and the glint of humor in his eyes that never seemed to fade, even when he spoke of his hardships. In return, I shared my aspirations and deep longing for a world beyond the confines of our war-stricken city.

What struck me most was his perspective on life. Despite the despair surrounding us, he always found beauty in the most minor things: a blooming flower amid the rubble, the laughter of children playing in the distance, the serene moonlight breaking through the gloom of night. He reminded me to appreciate these moments and to hold onto hope. Our meetings became the highlight of my days. We would sit under the same window where we first met, talking for hours. Sometimes, it was just comfortable silence, watching the world go by. During these moments, I realized I was beginning to see him in a different light. He was no longer just the persistent soldier who stood under my window. He had become a significant part of my life.

Love, I learned, can blossom in the most unexpected places. It didn't need grand gestures or perfect timing. Sometimes, it just needed two people willing to find solace in each other amidst the turmoil. Our relationship became a sanctuary, a haven where we could escape the dread of our city. As the days passed, our bond deepened, transforming into a love that was as surprising as it was profound. This unexpected chapter of my life taught me that love is not weakened by adversity but often strengthened by it. It taught me that the most extraordinary stories sometimes begin with a simple "Hello" under a window.

A PROMISE IN THE WAR

Each day, as the sun began to set, casting long shadows over the battered streets, I would wait for him. True to his word, he came every day without fail. He always carried a quarter of a bread loaf in his hands, a simple yet profound gesture. It was his way of ensuring I had something to eat, a piece of his care and concern made tangible. In times when food was scarce, this gesture meant more than just sustenance, it was a symbol of shared hardship and mutual support.

Our city, ravaged by war, was a place where precariousness reigned. The constant threat loomed over us, a dark cloud that seemed never to lift. Yet, a different kind of certainty emerged in these moments with him. As he handed me the bread, his eyes would meet mine, and he would say, "Sleep without worries tonight. I am on duty, and while I'm there, no enemy will enter this city." His words were more than just a reassurance of safety. They were a promise of protection, a vow that he would do everything in his power to shield me, to keep the horrors of war at bay.

Despite the chaos that surrounded our lives, our relationship became a beacon of hope and stability. The war continued relentlessly, each day a gamble of survival. Yet, amid this endless turmoil, our bond grew more assertive. We found comfort and strength in each other's presence, a quiet resilience that defied the despair around us.

For us, this period wasn't just about falling in love but about finding a companion in the darkest times. It was about two souls clinging to each other, finding light in a world that had turned overwhelmingly dark. As we navigated the extreme doubt and fear, our connection deepened, laying the foundation for a journey just beginning. This wasn't just the start of a romance. It was the beginning of a shared story of endurance, hope, and the power of human connection in the face of adversity.

JUST THE START OF THE BEGINNING

As the war raged on outside our fragile sanctuary, our bond flourished against all odds. Each day he came to me, each loaf of bread he brought, and each promise he made to keep me safe stitched a deeper connection between us. In these moments, amidst the chaos, we found an unspoken understanding and a shared resilience. His nightly assurances, "Sleep without worries, I am on duty," became a mantra of hope and safety in my heart. It was more than just a soldier's vow; a lover pledged to guard not just the physical walls of our city but the fragile walls around my heart. In a world where tomorrow wasn't promised, his words were a soothing balm to the constant fear and anxiety that plagued our days.

Our relationship, forged and tempered in the fires of war, was a rare bloom in a desolate landscape. We were two souls finding light in each other, a flicker of joy in a sea of sorrow. With his unwavering strength and humor, he brought a sense of normalcy and hope to my life. And I, in return, offered him a haven of warmth and understanding.

We created a small pocket of peace in a world torn apart by conflict.

As we faced each day, hand in hand, we understood that what we had was unique, a bond that was not just about the love blossoming between us but also about the strength we drew from each other. This wasn't merely the commencement of a love story but the beginning of a journey of mutual support and endurance. Amidst the backdrop of war, our love story was beginning, and that story will be a witness of the enduring power of love in the darkest of times.

EMBRACING DESTINY IN THE CHAOS

It felt like destiny was weaving its intricate tapestry in my life. The journey that led me away from Sarajevo in search of my mother only to bring me back to the same place, was nothing short of a twist of fate. In this city, marked by the scars of war, I found something unexpected: a connection that defied the tumultuous world around us.

At first, I had resisted his advances, guarded and skeptical. But as the reality of our situation sank in, the relentless war showing no signs of abating, the specter of death looming over us, it became clear that our time might be painfully short. We made a conscious decision, perhaps defiant against the cruelty of our circumstances, to seize the moment.

We decided to be teenagers, if only for a while, deliberately pushing the horrors of war to the back of our minds. It was a choice to embrace life in its purest form and indulge in the joy and naiveté our youth afforded us. In each other's company, we found an escape, a reprieve from the relentless sirens and the echoing gunshots. We laughed, shared stories, and dreamt of a future that seemed both impossible and distant under the starlit sky of Sarajevo. It was a bubble of normalcy, fragile and precious. Within this bubble, we allowed ourselves to explore the feelings blossoming between us, to relish the excitement and sweetness of a love that, under normal circumstances, would have been a typical rite of passage.

In those moments, we weren't just survivors of a brutal conflict; we were just two young souls discovering the thrills and spills of teenage romance. The ever-present war faded into a distant murmur, overshadowed by the laughter and warmth we found in each other. It was a bold rebellion against our reality, a choice to live, love, and dream, even when the world around us was falling apart. Though shadowed by the grim backdrop of war, the light of youthful love and hope brightened this chapter of my life. It witnessed the endurance of the human spirit and our innate desire to find happiness and connection, even in the darkest times.

Destiny was at play, leading me to a love that became my sanctuary, my moment of peace in a world of chaos.

BONDS FORGED IN SHADOWS

As the winter of 1994 blanketed Sarajevo in its cold embrace, a new chapter began in the war's relentless shadow. In these bleak and unsure times, I found an unexpected glimmer of hope in the form of companionship. The man I met under such dire circumstances had become an inseparable part of my life. Three months had passed since that fateful encounter, and in that short span, our bond had deepened, offering solace amidst the chaos.

February of 1994 marked a turning point. We decided to get married, not with the grandeur of a celebration, but through a mutual understanding and commitment to face whatever lay ahead together.

The war raged on around us, its end as unpredictable as the path it had carved through our lives. We had no ceremony, no exchange of rings, just a simple agreement that bound us in matrimony. It was a decision made not out of romance but necessity, a way to cling to a semblance of normalcy in a world turned upside down.

Elizabeta & Bejto
Sarajevo, Bosnia – February 1994

Each day was a struggle for survival, the war showing no signs of relenting. He, now my husband, still a soldier then, would share a quarter of the loaf of bread provided for his army lunch. This small, seemingly insignificant act became a symbol of our shared existence, of the life we were trying to sustain together. I no longer shared this meager ration with my sisters, as they had found their means of survival, but it was enough for us.

As the days turned into weeks and the weeks into months, we found strength in each other's presence. The war continued to rage around us, each day bringing new challenges and new fears. But during this turmoil, we discovered small joys and moments of peace. The sound of his footsteps became the highlight of my day. But as the winter slowly began to thaw, revealing the scars of the city beneath, our lives were about to change in a way we could never have anticipated. Amidst the danger, we faced a new reality that would add another layer to our struggle for survival.

With its relentless grip on Sarajevo, the war shaped our lives in countless ways. It had taken so much from us, yet it had also given us something precious in a twist of fate. We were about to embark on a journey that neither of us had foreseen, one that would test our resilience and commitment in ways we could never have imagined. As the sun set on another day of conflict and survival, we sat together in the dim light of our shelter, contemplating the future.

Then, I realized the total weight of the news we had just received, a revelation that would change our lives forever.

A LIGHT IN THE DARKNESS

During the relentless siege that had consumed Sarajevo, a surprising twist of fate emerged, piercing through the veil of despair and hardship that had become our daily reality. The war, with its unyielding cruelty, had stripped us of so much our home, our family, our sense of security. Yet, in this abyss of struggle, a new spark of hope flickered to life, a beacon amidst the darkness of our existence. As the weeks of war turned into months, each day a relentless fight for survival, my husband and I discovered that our lives were about to change profoundly. Amidst the hunger, the fear, and the uncertainty, we were about to become parents. This realization was both terrifying and exhilarating. It posed a question that hung heavily in the air: was this a cruel joke played by destiny, or was it a sign, a promise of better days ahead?

This new chapter in our lives brought a renewed determination to endure. The thought of bringing a child into a world ravaged by war was daunting, yet it also ignited a fierce resolve within us. The hunger pangs we had grown accustomed to took on a new meaning. It was no longer just about our survival; we had a new life to nurture, and to protect. The gravity of our situation weighed heavily on us. The reality of raising a child in a war was a daunting prospect.

Once a city of cultural richness and diversity, Sarajevo had become a battlefield, its streets echoing with gunfire and explosions. The daily struggle to find food and safe shelter was hard enough for us, but the thought of subjecting a child to such harsh conditions was unbearable. It became clear that we had to make a decision that seemed impossible under the circumstances. We had to leave Bosnia to find a safe place where we could raise our child away from the horrors of war. This decision was fraught with risk.

Leaving Sarajevo, a city under siege, was a dangerous endeavor. Yet, the prospect of a new life, a life free from the constant threat of violence, gave us the courage to contemplate this daunting journey.

As we planned our escape, each step was full of apprehension and hope. The war taught us the importance of holding onto hope and the value of resilience even in the darkest times. Our unborn child became a symbol of new beginnings and the driving force behind our resolve. We clung to the belief that somewhere, beyond the confines of a war-torn country, there was a place of peace, a world where our child could grow without the shadow of conflict looming overhead.

This impending parenthood, amidst the chaos of war, was a paradoxical blend of fear and hope. It compelled us to look beyond the immediate dangers and hardships to envision a future where survival was not the only goal but where living a life filled with love, safety, and opportunity was possible. Our road of escape, fraught with challenges and uncertainties, was about to begin. But with each step, we carried with us the promise of new life, a beacon of hope in the storm that had engulfed our lives.

******

JOURNEY TOWARDS HOPE

As the war in Bosnia continued to ravage the land we called home, we decided to leave Bosnia and seek refuge in Switzerland. This was a country known for its prosperity and stability, seemed like a beacon of hope amid the chaos surrounding us. The plan was for my husband to go first, paving the way for me to follow. The separation was painful, but it was a sacrifice we were willing to make for a chance at a safer life.

After my husband left, the lack of communication left me anxious. Yet, there was no turning back. Two months after he left it was time for me to embark on my journey. This was a path filled with unknowns and dangers but driven by the hope of a better future. My journey was solitary and arduous. I mainly traveled on foot, moving from village to village, driven by an unwavering determination.

The physical exhaustion was challenging, but the emotional toll was even more daunting. There were moments of overwhelming despair when hunger and fatigue would take their toll, and I would find myself stopping to cry. But these moments of vulnerability were always followed by a resurgence of strength, a reminder that there was no going back, only forward.

Crossing into Croatia marked a significant milestone. It was a tangible sign of progress, a step closer to my destination. In Croatia, I faced a critical part of my journey: boarding a bus to Zagreb without a ticket. The risk was high, but it was a necessary gamble. I sat quietly in the back, hoping to go unnoticed. This bus ride was more than just a means of transportation; it was a leap of faith, a step towards reuniting with my husband and starting anew. As the bus journeyed towards Zagreb, I reflected on the journey. Each step, each mile traversed, was a witness to my resilience and the unwavering hope that fueled me. The landscape outside the bus window was a blur, a symbol of the transient nature of our lives in these times of conflict.

Upon arriving in Zagreb, the sense of achievement was palpable. Despite the challenges, I had made it this far. The city was a waypoint, a brief pause in the longer journey towards Switzerland. As I disembarked, I felt a mix of relief and anticipation. The journey was far from over, but each step brought me closer to my husband, safety, and the possibility of a new beginning. This chapter of my journey was marked by solitude but also a period of profound personal growth. I learned about my strength, the depths of my determination, and the unbreakable spirit that sustains us through the most challenging times.

The road ahead was still long and uncertain, but I was ready to face it, driven by the promise of a reunion and the hope of a peaceful life in a new land.

THE ROAD TO FREEDOM

Zagreb greeted me with a tranquility that felt surreal. The absence of war's gunfire, and explosions was a balm to my weary soul. It contradicted the horrifying scenes I had left behind in Bosnia. With its serene streets and peaceful ambiance, this city offered a brief but much-needed respite. However, my relief was tempered by the reality of my situation. My pockets were empty, my resources limited to a single phone number. With trepidation, I made the call and arranged a pick-up, a small yet significant step in my journey. The plan was to spend the night in Zagreb and keep going forward in the morning.

That night in Zagreb, I was overwhelmed by the whirlwind of emotions. There was relief, certainly, but also an overwhelming sense of exhaustion. The physical toll of the journey had been immense, and doubts began to creep into my mind. Was I strong enough to continue? Could I make it to Switzerland, to freedom, and a new life?

An excerpt from my pocket phone book:

"I slept here for two nights. I won't have to stay longer, will I? I'm really fed up with everything. I can't take it anymore. I'm not the best with my health either. I'm writing and thinking, will "this man" come to pick me up tonight to take me away from here."

An excerpt from my pocket phone book:

"Zagreb, April 28th, 1995. 2:35pm. No one has come to get me. I lost all hopes. And when I get there, I don't know what to do. The worst part, I don't have money anymore. The road is long, and if I ever leave from here, I don't know if I will get there alive. This is already 4th day since I am in Zagreb."

These doubts haunted me for days as I remained in Zagreb, gathering strength for the next leg of my journey. With its calm and order, the city provided a space for introspection and recovery. But with each passing day, the urge to move forward, to continue my quest for freedom, grew more assertive. The most daunting part of the journey lay ahead, crossing the border on foot. This phase was fraught with risks and danger, yet it was a necessary passage towards the life that awaited me. As I prepared to leave Zagreb, I bolstered my resolve with thoughts of what lay ahead: freedom, a reunion with my husband, and the promise of a new beginning.

With each step toward the border, my determination solidified. The physical exhaustion, the hunger, the fear — the singular focus on my goal overshadowed all. The journey was more than just a physical trek; it tested my will, resilience, and unwavering desire for a better life. Crossing the border was not just a geographical milestone; it symbolized a crossing into a new phase of my life. Each step took me closer to my dreams, to the hopes I harbored for a peaceful existence far from the horrors of war. In my mind's eye, I visualized the life that awaited me, a life of safety, stability, and the chance to rebuild what was lost.

As I traversed the landscape, my thoughts often drifted back to Bosnia, my family, and the life I had left behind. These reflections were bittersweet, tinged with sadness for what was lost, yet hopeful for the future. The journey was arduous, but I felt a growing sense of accomplishment and anticipation with each mile covered.

This chapter of my life was a confirmation of my spirit's capacity for endurance and hope. Despite the challenges and the uncertainties, my journey toward freedom continued, driven by the belief that a better life waits for me beyond the border.

JOURNEY OF TWO

In the early spring of my journey, the weather graced me with its mildness. The air was fresh, and the sun's warmth was a gentle reprieve from the cold nights I had endured. However, the physical comfort provided by the weather was overshadowed by a more profound, more pressing concern: hunger. As I walked, a precious life grew within me, a secret companion on this arduous trek toward freedom. Seven months into my pregnancy, my body showed little sign of the life it nurtured. The scarcity of food meant that my unborn child was deprived of the nourishment needed for growth. This realization weighed heavily on me. My primary concern shifted from my survival to the well-being of the child I carried.

Each step I took was fueled by the desire for freedom and the maternal instinct to protect and provide for my unborn baby. The knowledge that I was responsible for another life provided a strength I didn't know I possessed. Amidst the physical exhaustion and the gnawing hunger, I found the strength to keep moving. As I traversed the landscape, my mind was filled with questions: "Where am I getting my strength from?" I would wonder. There were moments when I felt like I was on the brink of my physical and emotional limits. Yet, each time I felt like giving up, the thought of my unborn child spurred me on. "How much longer?" became a recurring thought, a reflection of both my anticipation and anxiety.

The closer I got to my destination, the more my concerns became pressing. I wasn't asking for much, just shelter, some food, and the necessities to ensure the health of my unborn child. The urgency of these needs pushed me to avoid stopping, to keep moving despite the weariness that clung to my every step. This journey was more than a physical voyage; it was a journey of hope, resilience, and maternal love. The unpredictability of my situation, the concern for my unborn child, and the longing for a shelter all merged into a singular driving force. Each day brought challenges, but with every passing hour, I was getting closer to my destination, to the promise of safety and a new beginning for me and my child.

The strength I found during this journey came from the power of a mother's love and determination. Despite the odds, I was determined to reach a place where I could provide for my child and to ensure their safety and well-being. This journey was not just for my freedom but to secure a future for the life that grew within me.

*****

ARRIVAL AND ASYLUM

After a harrowing trek filled with fear and immense physical strain, I arrived at the designated pickup location. The relief of knowing I no longer had to walk, that I was finally at the threshold of a new beginning, was overwhelming. There, I was met by my husband and his sister, who had already established a life in Switzerland. Their familiar faces were like beacons of hope during the chaos that had become my life. They understood the complexities of my situation and the delicate balance between relief and legality. As I crossed the Swiss border, I knew I had entered the country illegally. This realization brought a mix of emotions: relief at having reached safety and apprehension about the legal implications of my arrival.

The decision to turn ourselves into the authorities was a calculated one. After years of being a displaced person within my own country, I was about to claim the status of a refugee officially. My husband, who had shared in the ordeals of displacement and the quest for safety, stood by me as we presented ourselves to the Swiss authorities. It was a moment that signified the end of one journey and the beginning of another.

The Swiss authorities processed our case with a level of efficiency and humanity that was both unexpected and deeply appreciated. We were escorted to a refugee shelter, a temporary home offering stability and safety. The shelter was a far cry from the dangers and hesitancy we had faced, but it was also a stark reminder of our status: refugees, displaced, and dependent on the goodwill of a foreign nation.

Adjusting to life in the shelter brought its own set of challenges. The environment was unfamiliar, and the reality of being a refugee in a foreign land was a constant undercurrent in our daily lives. Despite these challenges, there was an undeniable sense of gratitude. I was grateful for the safety we had found, the opportunity to start anew, and the chance to bring our child into a world far removed from the chaos and destruction of war.

In this new chapter, my husband and I faced the future with hope, determination, and resilience. Our journey taught us the value of perseverance, the strength of the human spirit, and the power of hope. As refugees in Switzerland, we were embarking on a path filled with ambiguity, but we were together, and after everything we had endured, that was a victory.

Our story, made from loss, survival, and new beginnings, was far from over. But as we settled into our temporary home in the refugee shelter, we held onto the belief that better days lay ahead and that our struggles would pave the way for a future filled with peace and stability for our family.

A NEW LIFE BEGINS

June 1995 brought a transformation into my life, a glimmer of hope in the form of a new beginning. Amidst the backdrop of our struggles as refugees, a new life emerged. I gave birth to a beautiful little girl, symbolizing resilience, hope, and the promise of a brighter future. The first news I received about her was concerning. She was too small, they said. My heart sank as I remembered the countless days during my journey when I went without food, the days of walking, the stress, and the fear. All these factors had taken their toll, not just on me but, unwittingly, on her too. But the moment I looked at her, all my fears dissolved into a profound sense of awe and love. This tiny, precious being, so fragile yet full of life, was here because of my journey.

Holding her in my arms, I felt an overwhelming sense of responsibility and purpose. She was more than just a child; she was the reason for the journey I had undertaken. A journey that spanned what felt like half the world. Every step I had taken, every hardship I had endured, was worth it for this moment. I had walked through war, traversed borders, and faced countless dangers, all to bring this little girl safely into the world.

In her, I saw a new hope, a fresh start not just for her but for our entire family. We were safe now, away from the conflict and the instability that had marked so many years of our lives. Her birth in a peaceful country, far from the ravages of war, symbolized a break from our past and the beginning of a new chapter.

This new life in my arms was a beacon of hope, a reminder that even in the darkest times, life can find a way to continue, to thrive. She represented all the possibilities ahead, all the dreams and aspirations that now could be realized. Looking down at her tiny face, I silently vowed to provide her with all the love, safety, and opportunities I could. She would grow up in a world far from the one I had known, where the sounds of gunfire and the fear of war were replaced by the laughter of children and the promise of a peaceful future.

The little girl, born in a foreign land to refugee parents, symbolized resilience, and hope. She was a reminder that even during upheaval and uncertainty, life continues, bringing new beginnings and the promise of a better tomorrow.

******

CROSSROADS OF DESTINY

As months rolled into a year and a half, our life in the Swiss refugee shelter became a monotonous echo of uncertainty. Initially a haven, the shelter gradually turned into a cramped mosaic of faces from around the globe, each carrying their own story of escape and hope. This diversity, while enriching, also underscored a growing feeling of alienation. I began to feel like an outsider, longing for an increasingly elusive sense of belonging.

The shelter's walls started to feel more like barriers. They confined not just our physical space but also seemed to limit our prospects for the future. Amidst this crowd of strangers, I yearned for the familiarity of family, for the comfort of a home where my daughter could grow and thrive. My heart ached for my family back in Sarajevo. Their absence was a constant reminder of the life we had left behind. While initially fascinating, the constant buzz of different languages and the different cultures converging in this one place began to weigh heavily on me. I felt like a permanent outsider, unable to integrate or find my footing fully. The sense of not belonging gnawed at me, planting seeds of restlessness and despair.

As I watched my daughter grow each day in this environment of transience, a resolve began to stir within me. I couldn't let this be her future. She deserved stability, a place to call home, an environment where she could form lasting bonds and create her identity.

The end of the war in Bosnia brought a new dilemma to the forefront of my mind. Should I return to the land where I grew up, a place now free from conflict but scarred by the memories of war? Or should I venture further, seek a new beginning in a different land, even further, one that promised better opportunities for my daughter and us? This decision loomed over me, a crossroads that held the key to our future and the essence of our past. Returning to Bosnia meant confronting the ghosts of our past, rebuilding amidst the remnants of a life that once was. On the other hand, venturing into a new country meant starting from scratch, embracing the unknown, and possibly finding the acceptance and opportunities we desperately sought.

As I pondered this critical decision, I ultimately felt helpless. The choice was not just about geography. It was about finding a place where we could heal, grow, and belong. With its ever-changing faces and stories, the shelter was a constant reminder that our current situation was not a destination but a mere stopover on our journey. The questions that haunted me was about where to go and who we would become in the process. Each option carried its challenges and possibilities, and a promise of a future yet to be written.

And so, as the twilight of one chapter approached, the dawn of another beckoned, filled with hope and the promise of a new beginning. The decision I was about to make would not just shape our lives but also define our legacy. It was a choice between returning to our roots or branching into new horizons.

ECHOES OF WAR
AND
WHISPERS OF LOVE

As I look back on the tumultuous tapestry of my youth in Sarajevo, I see not just a narrative of war and love but also family, my mother, my brothers, and two sisters, integral threads in the fabric of my story. With its relentless shadows, the war had brought us closer, binding us in our shared struggle for survival. In this struggle, an unexpected chapter unfolded, a tender love that blossomed in the unlikeliest of time.

My mother, a pillar of strength and resilience, taught us the power of hope. Even in the face of danger, her unwavering spirit was a constant source of inspiration. My sisters, each in their way, contributed to the tapestry of our lives during the war. My middle sister, who unknowingly became the bridge to my unexpected encounter with a skinny soldier whose heart was full of humor and hope. As I navigated the complexities of a wartime romance, my family was my anchor. They witnessed my transformation from a girl hardened by the cruelties of war to someone who dared to love amid despair. Their support gave me the courage to embrace this unexpected joy. This chapter of my life, marked by the echoes of war and the whispers of love, is a witness to our resilience. It taught me that even when the world is falling apart, the bonds of family and the power of love can create something beautiful and enduring.

As I am writing down these memories, I realize this is more than my story. It is a story of a family that survived the unthinkable, found strength in each other, and discovered that even in the darkest nights, stars can still shine brightly. It is a narrative woven with loss and love, a reminder that during life's most brutal storms, we can find shelter in the hearts of those we call family.

This memoir is a reflection on war, love, and family,
and it is a tribute to those I lost and those who stood by me.

Author is the owner of the image "Sisters."
Foca, Bosnia – Summer 1991

SHADOWS OF HISTORY: UNDERSTANDING THE WAR IN SARAJEVO

As I recount the days spent in the labyrinth of Sarajevo's war-torn streets, I realize the importance of painting the broader strokes of history, as these events did not occur in isolation. Instead, they were part of a complex and tragic tapestry woven into the very fabric of the Balkans. The war in Bosnia and Herzegovina was rooted in a blend of historical, political, and cultural factors. Yugoslavia, once a federation of six republics, began to unravel with the fall of communism in Eastern Europe. Nationalism surged among various ethnic groups, leading to a quest for independence that ignited tensions in a region already fraught with historical conflicts. Bosnia and Herzegovina, with its diverse population of Bosniaks, Serbs, and Croats, became a unity of this larger struggle.

For Bosnia, the declaration of independence from Yugoslavia in 1992 meant a new beginning. Instead, it marked the onset of a brutal conflict fueled by ethnic divisions and external influences. Sarajevo, the capital, encapsulated the heart of Bosnia's multicultural ethos. A city known for its unique blend of Eastern and Western cultures, where mosques, churches, and synagogues stood side by side, became the epicenter of a siege that lasted from 1992 to 1995. It was one of the longest sieges in modern warfare, a period marked by constant shelling, sniper attacks, and a dire shortage of food, water, and essential supplies.

The impact of the war on the people of Sarajevo and Bosnia was profound. It was not just a battle over territory but an assault on the very identity and spirit of the region. Neighbors turned against neighbors, and the city, once a symbol of diversity and coexistence, was scarred by divisions and loss. As a young person living through this turmoil, the war was both a personal tragedy and a lesson in the complexities of human nature. It taught me about the resilience required to survive not just the physical destruction but also the emotional and psychological toll of such conflict. The war was a relentless shadow that loomed over every aspect of our lives, shaping our daily experiences, relationships, and outlook on life.

In sharing my story, it is important to acknowledge this historical context to understand that our struggles were part of a larger narrative of a region grappling with its identity, past, and future. This understanding is vital for anyone looking to grasp the full impact of the war in Bosnia and Herzegovina. This war was about the territory, the soul of a people, and the heart of a country that once stood proudly as a beacon of multicultural harmony.

******

EPILOGUE: EMBERS OF HOPE IN THE ASHES OF WAR

As I reflect upon the journey that my life has taken, from the bustling streets of my childhood neighborhood in Foca, to the stark and dangerous paths of a war-torn country, I am overwhelmed by the resilience of the human spirit. The war in Bosnia, a conflict that ripped apart our lives, taught me lessons in survival, love, and the importance of hope in the darkest times.

Through the chaos and the fear, the loss of my beloved brothers, and the countless hardships we faced emerged strength I never knew I possessed. In the embrace of my makeshift family in the basements and classrooms in Sarajevo and in the eyes of my husband, who stood by my side, I found the courage to continue each day. Our decision to leave Bosnia, propelled by the arrival of our child, was one of the most difficult choices I ever made. To leave behind the land that held the memories of my childhood, my family, and the obstacles we had overcome was to leave a part of myself behind. But the instinct to protect our future, to provide a life of peace and safety for our child, outweighed the pain of leaving. Years later, as I sit in the serenity of my new home, far from the Echoes of War, I realize that my journey was not only about survival. It demonstrated the enduring power of love and family, the importance of holding onto hope, and the unbreakable bond of shared experiences.

This memoir is not just my story. It is a tribute to those who stood with me, those we lost, and the countless others who have lived through similar events. It is a reminder that even amid the devastation, the human spirit can thrive, and new beginnings can emerge from the ashes of despair. To my readers, let this memoir serve as a reminder of the resilience within all of us. May it inspire you to find strength in your hardships and to always hold onto hope. In our darkest moments, the light of our spirit shines the brightest.

A TRIBUTE:
TO THE CHILDREN IN WAR

At the end of my story, I'd like to pay tribute to all the

children who we lost in wars.

You will be remembered forever.

Rest in peace my angels.

To those who still fight for existence, you are not alone.

The End.